Under the Stars

Under the Stars

THE LIFE AND TIMES
OF
TOM TEPPER

Tom Tepper
as told to
Nancy Bringhurst

RiverWood Books
ASHLAND, OREGON

Printed in Korea

First edition: 2004

Cover design: David Rupee, Impact Publications

Library of Congress Cataloging-in-Publication Data
Tepper, Tom.
Under the stars : the life and times of Tom Tepper / by Tom
Tepper ; as told to Nancy Bringhurst.-- 1st ed.
p. cm.
ISBN 1-883991-86-2
1. Tepper, Tom. 2. Ranch life--Oregon. 3. Air pilots--Oregon--
Biography. 4. Carpenters--Oregon--Biography. 5. Businessmen--
Oregon--Biography. 6 --Oregon--Biography. I. Bringhurst, Nancy. II.
Title

CT275.T435A3 2003
973.91'092--dc21
[B]
2003046589

CONTENTS

To Elva Brunner Tepper
for her love and support
in countless ways.

Meeting Tom Tepper

I agreed to stop in Shady Cove that day, but not because I wanted to especially. I was being polite. What I wanted to do was see Crater Lake. Ever since we'd begun commuting from the East Coast to build a house in the mountains in Oregon, we'd been told we had to see the deepest lake in the country. Crater Lake is nearly two thousand feet deep and sits in a six-mile-wide caldera, a souvenir from the Mount Mazama eruption that spewed its fury as far away as Canada around seven thousand years ago. Finally, we'd carved a day out of our week, normally pressured with things like tile and window selections, and we were on our way to Crater Lake. Besides, it was a summer day, the kind meant to be spent outside under the cool conifer canopy.

However, we had friends visiting from Pennsylvania, and Tepper's violin wood was part of the reason they had come in the first place. Enticed by an advertisement in Connoisseur Magazine, they wanted to see this family-run business where they could buy wood for her brother, an architect and violin maker in London. They were our guests, so I could hardly refuse them a brief stop, especially since we went right through Shady Cove on the way. Only it wasn't brief.

We drove down a long road that used to lead to a ferry that for years provided the only means of crossing the Rogue River in that area, unless you went by horseback. But that was a dangerous thing to do years ago, especially when the thirty-to forty-pound salmon were running, their slippery bodies covering every square inch of the river. In 1928 a flood snatched the ferry and took it careening down the Rogue River through Hell's Canyon, eventually spitting it out into the ocean at Gold Beach, where it turned south and came to rest at last in Crescent City. Several years later an official with a sense of humor wrote to the folks in Shady Cove saying he had their ferry in Crescent City and in what manner did they wish to have it returned. By then a bridge was solidly in place, and probably few people missed the runaway ferry anyway. So now the road dead-ends at the Teppers' instead of the ferry landing.

Their three-family compound was sandwiched between the river and the base of a mountain. It was where Tom and Elva and two of their three sons lived and worked. Houses, outbuildings, machinery, and various sorts of cars, trucks, motorcycles, and dirt bikes were scattered around. There was an airplane in the process of being built by Tim, their youngest son. There were even the rusty remains of an old red and white plane they had salvaged from a wreck years before. Narrow dirt roads wove through in a network of connections.

John was expecting us. John is their middle son, and he runs the business their father started in 1970. He took us on a tour that eventually brought us to the pristine, library-like site where the wood was stored neatly, according to its future use, in narrow vertical shelving: big leaf maple and spruce wood waiting to be miraculously transformed into the violins, violas, cellos, and basses to be played by some of the world's finest musicians.

Before that day I'd never given a single thought to the making of a violin. "How many trees do you cut down a year?" I asked.

"We average two or three a year," John answered, "but the most my dad and I ever took was seven in one year."

John mentioned his father frequently, so when he asked if we'd like to meet him, we nodded eagerly. My interest in Tom Tepper and his life and work was gaining momentum, and the thought of Crater Lake slowly receding. John pointed us in the direction of the log house Tom and his wife had built in 1962, and off he went to collect his father from the workshop, where Tom spent most of his time making walking sticks, carvings, tools, and whatever else he felt like creating. We waited for them outside, speculating about a bed perched just to the right of the house on the bank of the river. It was an ordinary bed with sheets and blankets on it and a make-shift canopy attached. Only this was no ordinary bedroom.

Our curiosity was interrupted by their arrival, and we were invited in. Tom reminded me of a well-mannered cat: shy, fiercely independent, happy for attention, but clearly the one deciding from whom he will accept it and to whom he will give it. He was the loner-cat sort, one who would rather spend his time in solitude than with others not of his own choosing. Tom was obviously uncomfortable with the friendly hugs passed around so liberally, but there was a genuine warmth and spirit of generosity that filled the room when he entered. At that time Tom could practically run up the mountain trails. He was alert, meticulously observant, and even suspicious, quietly scrutinizing the motives of strangers he ran across on his land, or met in the back country. He was quiet in his move-ments, careful and graceful. Yet one got the feeling he could leap into action if necessary. He had spent most of his life outside, and he didn't like it one bit now that age called him in more and more. That bed we saw outside was the bed he had been sleeping in for the last twenty-five years, through all four seasons, through sleet, snow, and thunderstorms.

Just inside the door, propped in the corner, was a huge collec-tion of walking sticks. On the walls hung a variety of wood carv-ings, mostly of delicate flowers with three-dimensional petals. A small bed, spread with piles of quilting material, stood just to the right of the door. Beside the bed stood a dining table that obvi-ously served as much for a desk as for eating. Bookshelves and stacks of magazines and papers piled everywhere dwarfed the small tele-vision set. The main focus of the room was a large picture window with a perfectly framed view of the Rogue River with its white wa-ter and occasional rafters rushing by.

The introductions were barely over when Tom told us he was almost eighty and one of his hips had been replaced. "Can you guess which one?" he asked. He jumped in the air, spun around one hundred and eighty degrees, landed on his feet, and did a little jig.

We admired the walking sticks, and I asked if I could buy one.

"I don't sell them," he said, "I only give them to people I like. That way I don't have people I don't like walking around with my sticks." I was embarrassed and wished I hadn't opened my mouth. "Would you like to have one?" he asked.

Today we have an array of walking sticks propped in the entrance to our house in Oregon. "Here, try this out," Tom would say, handing us yet another beautiful one. "I changed the top a little and I think it'll fit better in your hand." Or he would hand us two or three and ask, "Which of these wood grains do you like best? I'm trying something new." It was never an easy choice.

Tom and I exchanged letters for a few months before I had the chance to return. His letters read like mini lectures in dendrology and outdoor survival. They were refreshing, and made me eager to see him again. As my husband and I drove to Shady Cove for our second visit, he said, "Now I don't want to stay long. I think an hour will be long enough." A typical clock-watching New Yorker, that man.

Tom met us at the door and it was obvious he was alone. When I asked if we would meet his wife, he said, "Oh, Elva's canned some peaches and she's taking them around to give them to her friends."

My husband and I sat together on the sofa, and Tom began to talk as if we'd always known each other. I worried about my husband, though. A man used to topics like price/earning ratios, the Dow Jones Industrial Average, and current interest rates is not likely to sit still very long listening to how the Douglas fir came to be called Pseudotsuga menziesii instead of Pseudotsuga taxifolia, or about the potential germination of seed lots. Yet I was the one who, four hours later, suggested that maybe we should be on our way. I had hinted several times before, but my husband ignored me completely and stayed glued to the couch. It wasn't that I wanted to leave. It was just that I didn't want a grumbling, complaining husband for the rest of the day, a martyr saying, "I only did it for you."

"That was like an exciting seminar," he said as we waved goodbye and pulled out of the driveway. It was a seminar given by a man who never went beyond eighth grade. We had been treated to a wealth of technical information on the tree seed business, the violin wood business, silver making techniques, and flying, as well as true and exciting stories of the West, a history of Oregon, and

View of the Rogue River from the Tepper home.

Tom and Elva's bed outside their door by the river where they slept many years—rain, shine, or snow. Even lightning storms wouldn't drive Tom indoors. Deer would come and eat from Elva's hand.

John Tepper in their 'library' of music wood.

even poetry recitations. No wonder we didn't want to leave. Those four hours sent shock waves through my lazy brain cells. They must have sent gargantuan shock waves through my husband's gastronomic anatomy. He had forgotten lunch.

I couldn't stop thinking about Tom, though. I wanted to know more about the life he'd led and the many things he'd done to make him who he was. Here was a man who had broken wild horses, won prizes in rodeos, taught jewelry making, was a flight instructor in the Army Air Corps, crop dusted, fished commercially, designed and made tools, invented and made his own machinery for the tree seed business he started, made intricate wood carvings and found the wood that world renowned musicians had their violins and violas made from. Along with that, he was well read, he spoke like a college professor, and his gracious and courtly manners certainly didn't conjure up an image of a cowboy.

"Tom is a walking encyclopedia," an old friend of his told us five years after we met Tom. We met his friend Gordon Jesse Walker, a mule skinner, lecturer, and author, when he came to douse for water for a well for us.

"I first met Tom Tepper near Frye Creek, up on Parker Meadows Road where it parallels the south fork of the Rogue River," Walker said. "I came across this guy eating yew berries. 'Everyone

Intricate carvings designed and made by Tom.

thinks these berries are poisonous,' Tom said, 'and that's fine with me because it leaves all the more for me to eat.' So I started to eat them, too, and I'm still here.

"That's Tom," Walker told us. "He also taught me where to look for squirrel caches. When I asked if he could teach me to fly, he said, 'Oh, come on. We'll just get in the plane and you'll have it in no time.' He took me up over what we called the Dead Indian Country, southeast of Ashland. 'You can't do a thing to this plane that I can't pull us out of,' he reassured me. Suddenly he said, 'Looks like a lot of Shasta fir cones down there. Let's go have a look.' Next thing I knew we had swooped down and were just over the tree tops having a look. I decided right then and there that I didn't really want to fly after all. Oh, I've since flown many planes once they were in the air, but I never took off or landed one on my own. I tell you Tom Tepper was the best pilot I ever flew with. I don't think they come any better."

Chapter 1

Directions and Indicators

Tepper, stand up and apologize or walk out of that door and never come back." I walked out that door and never did go back to that school, or any other. I haven't had a single regret. The following spring, 1924, my father bought a second-hand 23 Ford Model T. The two of us climbed in and headed West. I was thirteen and never had I been so happy.

Well, that's not altogether true. I was happy when my brother John was alive. We were inseparable. John was sixteen months older, and everything I learned had been with my brother by his side. Then one summer evening, John complained he didn't feel well. By morning he was worse. The doctor prescribed medicine, but it did no good. "Summer pneumonia," the doctor said. John died around midnight, and I was completely lost for a long time to come.

Both of us were born in our mother's family house in Millburn, New Jersey, where we lived until we moved to a farm near Gladstone, New Jersey. We loved that farm. We loved our sleeping loft under the roof, eating nuts from the hickory and butternut trees, fishing for minnows and sunfish, and exploring every corner of the place. It was impossible to be bored there.

Swimming was our favorite. Our father began to teach us to swim in our pond, promising to teach us more the following Sunday. A week was too far away for us though, and our own pond was much too small for our exuberance. What could we do but sneak off to a bigger and deeper neighboring pond that better fit our needs. John boldly announced his intention to swim across the pond

The Whittingham House in Milburn, New Jersey. Tom's first home.

Tom (second from the left, back row) in his father's Boy Scout Troop.
His father is sixth from the left, back row.

and back, so I, with typical young boy pride and sibling rivalry, boasted that I could certainly do the same. I did. At least twenty times. When the promised Sunday finally rolled around, our father offered to continue our lessons. He was taken aback when we offered to show him what we could already do, which put him in the position of having to choose between punishment and praise. He chose silence.

I often copied John, though not always as successfully. It was hard for us to resist playing with an old corn chopper near our farm, what with its large iron wheel connected to an iron shaft with two cogwheels. John cranked the wheel up, got it going fast, then put his finger on top of the cogwheels and declared how funny it felt. "Try it," he said to me, and I did. John spun the wheel, but accidentally spun it the wrong way, which made the cogs turn toward each other. I didn't get the same funny feeling that had pleased my brother. Instead, I got a thumb full of unbearable pain as it was pulled down between the wheels and crushed. The wheels stopped, but there was no way for me to get my thumb out, nor could anyone stop my howling. My mother and aunt came running, but they had no idea which way to turn the wheel, and fortunately they knew better than to try. The wrong way would have left me with no thumb at all. Luckily, there were workers in a nearby field, and though they couldn't speak a word of English, they could see what the problem was. They released my thumb, still attached but hanging by a thread, and that's how it stayed until my father came home several hours later and took me to the doctor.

We had five glorious years on the farm before moving to a three-story house above the small town of Millington, New Jersey. Our freedom came to a sad halt. We were surrounded by NO TRESPASSING signs and aggressive, unfriendly children who couldn't speak English. We were ready for school, but there was no school to go to. With the influx of Europeans coming to work in the factories, there were more children than there were schools to hold them. New Jersey State law required all children of eight years or over to report to and attend the nearest school, but the local townships or counties didn't have enough taxpayers to furnish money to build or run one.

The first day of school, my father took us to the local grade school, only to find the doors locked and the teachers inside with twelve or fifteen empty desks. Outside, there were at least seventy-five children waiting to get in. It took awhile before my parents found Mrs. Moody, a retired teacher from England, who agreed to teach about a dozen local children. Her classroom consisted of two sofas, put end to end, and two blackboards on the wall in her home. She would teach one class for an hour and then move on to the

Left: Tom (left) and John with their mother.

Three generations: Tom in his father's lap, and his brother John sitting in their grandfather Tepper's lap.

Tom's father's cattle round-up days.

next. Since Mrs. Moody refused to teach beyond the third grade, John and I spent our fourth and fifth grades with Reverend Ahrends in the local Episcopal Church. There were only five students in his class, which meant plenty of time for individual help. But Reverend Ahrends refused to teach beyond sixth grade, so once again we were without a school.

That summer, my father took us fishing and camping in Canada. World War I was just beginning, and the roads were filled with soldiers preparing to sail for France. We were traveling in a brand new passenger Cunningham—a bribe from the Acme Harrow Farm Machinery Company to keep my father from leaving. I can still see that car. Its clutch was a large lever on the left outside of the car. To put the acetylene headlights on, we had to turn on the cylinder, which was also on the outside of the car, swing the glass plate open, and strike a match to light it. Then we'd run around and do it on the other side. It gave off a yellowish light one could see for about fifty feet, but it was impossible to light in a rain or a strong wind.

That was John's last summer. He died the following year, and I only saw him one more time after that. I never told my parents though. I figured they'd think I'd gone crazy. It was during the time I was recuperating from scarlet fever. I'd been quarantined on the third floor of our house, just as John had been. For three or four days the high fever had kept me delirious. The fever finally broke. I was weak, but I was very coherent when I woke with a start a couple of night later and could see, just as clearly as I could see anything else—there, across the room, was my brother, kneeling and praying beside a little cot. He and the pajamas he was wearing were bright white and glistening. I sat up in my cot and looked right at him. Within seconds he and the cot disappeared. Much later I asked my mother where John was when he died. "In a little cot," she said, and described the location exactly as I had seen it.

Knowing more about my father makes it easy to understand how he could just pick up and move from New Jersey and homestead in Oregon. He was an accomplished mathematician, but he had always loved horses. At eighteen, he set off for New Mexico to be a cowboy. He rode for a large ranch for two years before pneumonia almost killed him. He would have died had his friends not put him in a wagon and driven all day and night to get him to the nearest doctor. After he recovered, he headed back east.

When the Spanish American War began, he and a group formed a cavalry unit, complete with their own horses, to join Theodore Roosevelt's Rough Rider group. My father won the squad marksmanship competition and was presented with a new .38 caliber Colt revolver engraved with his name and rank. (His namesake, my son Arthur, has that revolver today.) Their horses were loaded on a ship for Cuba, and the men were looking forward to their days of glory. But there was to be no sailing and no glory for them. News stopped them in their eagerness: The Spaniards had surrendered.

In 1900, my father met Hannah Harrison Whittingham. They were married four years later in Hot Springs, Colorado, where he was laying out bridges and trestles on the proposed Denver and Rio Grande Railroad to Leadville, Colorado. In New Jersey, my mother was used to a comfortable life with all the amenities, so it must have been a shock to find herself living that summer in a tent in the mountains, cooking on a wood stove, and riding in a four-wheeled buckboard instead of the luxury car she'd been used to. She seemed to manage just fine, but my father developed typhoid fever. She nursed him to a full recovery and they returned to the East Coast, where he found work laying out new piers for a dock on the Hudson River for the North German Lloyd Steamship Line.

I have a deep and well-deserved respect for my father for many reasons, but one example suffices. My father and a long-time acquaintance won a contract to build a new high school in Summit, New Jersey, with the agreement they would be paid half when the building was half completed. When they reached that stage, the school board had the work inspected and gave the promised payment to my father's partner—half of the total, a sizeable amount. His partner, a man known and trusted by all, cashed that check and disappeared with an eighteen-year-old girl, leaving his wife and children behind, destitute. He was never seen or heard from again. My father was left with nothing but a pile of debts and his ethics. Declaring bankruptcy was out of the question for him. He borrowed enough to pay all of the creditors, but there was no way he could continue building alone. He found work as a CPA, and that was when they had to sell the large family home in Millburn and move to the farm.

After John died, I was extremely lonely. He wasn't just my brother, he had been my best friend. Now I had no one to play with, and I missed the freedom to roam the countryside like we had on the farm. To make matters worse, that fall the school situation was critical. There were no schools and no qualified teachers nearby. My parents had no choice but to consider a boarding school for me. They rejected the first one we looked at, since it looked rather like a training camp for the army. They chose instead Saint Bernard's Episcopal Farm School for boys, about twenty miles from Millington, a school that took boys from grades five through eight. I called it "Saint Barnyards." It became my home for the next four years, and though the suppression wasn't up to army standards, it was not without its own kind of brutality, subtle as it was.

The general plan of the school had some merit though. We were well educated in the subjects taught in regular schools, and certainly anyone graduating from there could always make a living farming. We were taught self-reliance and how to cooperate with others. But there wasn't much enjoyment in the process. Mostly it was just plain hard work under the watchful eyes of extremely strict disciplinarians.

Each student had to earn a quarter of his tuition and board by working. A bell jarred us out of our sleep each morning while it was still pitch black, and we were required to do thirty minutes of chores before breakfast. After breakfast, half of the boys did chores outside until noon while the other half attended classes. After lunch, we swapped places. On Mondays, the shifts were rotated. There was milking to be done; eggs to be gathered; chickens, pigs, and horses to be fed; barns and chicken houses to be cleaned; and field corn and hay to be raised. Never mind zero-degree weather, snow past our boots, or howling winds—the work had to be done, thank you very much. The younger boys were assigned the job of filling a pail with milk and a basket with eggs and delivering them to the principal's house, which was no easy task in the dark with blinding snow or sleet pelting our faces. And, of course, there was punishment to pay if we were clumsy enough to break or spill the precious cargo. I dreaded most of all cleaning the chicken house.

The dust from sweeping choked me and the smell stuck to my clothes the rest of the day, which did not endear me to myself or anyone else.

The farm fields had deep rich soil, but each time they were plowed, hundreds of rocks would surface. It was our job to cart those rocks away. That was the nastiest job of all in the winter. We used a device called a stone boat. It was made from the crotch or fork of an oak tree cut about a foot and a half below the fork. The forks were cut about eight feet long above the crotch. Boards were nailed across the crotch, and a ring or chain was fastened to the end of the single piece. Laid flat, it made a sled that could be easily loaded and dragged to wherever it was needed. We'd load rocks on that stone boat for four hours, sometimes every day of the week. We were given no gloves, and our hands would get so chapped they'd become raw between our fingers. We were given no salve or ointment, only strange advice: Urinate on your hands. Would you believe it worked? Not right away, but within a few days our hands would heal.

After the evening meal, we were marched off to study hall for an hour, and then to a short service in the chapel before bedtime. Usually we had a reprieve from field work on weekends, with only general chores to do that took all morning. Sunday mornings we had to dress in our best clothes and walk a mile to the Episcopal Church in Gladstone. There we had to sit still for a boring two-hour-long service.

One Sunday, though, our boredom was broken by a little mouse intent on entertaining us by struggling to get across the stained glass window just behind the preacher's pulpit. He'd crawl a little way, leap for another foothold, and then go a little further. When he reached the middle of the window, he slipped and slid down about two feet, caught a foothold, and started on again. We all let out a "whew" when we saw him catch himself, and when he arrived safely on the other side we gave another big sigh of relief. The principal and our teachers didn't think it was one bit funny. In fact, they lectured us all week on the terrible blasphemy and sacrilege we'd committed in church by paying more attention to a mouse than to the preacher. It was this incident, along with other similar ones, that made me begin to question the merit of the religion I'd been raised to believe in, or any organized religion for that matter.

Each and every misdeed at the school exacted a penalty, but there was one that was exceptionally abhorrent. They had torn down a brick building on the school grounds and dumped the bricks in a huge pile. They were planning to erect a new building about two hundred yards away, and these bricks were being moved to the new site by the transgressors among students. For each form of misconduct, we were given a certain number of bricks: twenty-five bricks for one-hour penance, fifty bricks for two hours, etc. One hundred bricks took a huge chunk out of our precious little free time. The worst part was that it all had to be done on our one hour off after the midday meal. On top of that, there were rigidly enforced ways of toting those bricks. We could carry only one in each hand, we had to walk, as running was forbidden, and at the halfway mark we had to pile the bricks neatly in a rectangle in multiples of five. Once that was completed, we were compelled to stand there at attention until a teacher came to inspect what we'd done. Sometimes we stood for as long as twenty minutes, and then if the inspector found the pile too loose, he would push it over and demand it be piled again. Once we got the okay, we'd pick up a brick in each hand, go to the end, and pile them again. It was a dreary job for such young boys. I should know—I carried a lot of those bricks during my years there.

The food was plain, but usually good. Although we collected hundreds of eggs every day, only the principal, his wife, and the English teacher ate eggs each morning. The rest were sold, along with the cream. Though we went without eggs and cream, I remember the delicious fresh-bread baked in a wood stove oven each morning, and the Postum made from skim milk. There were eight or ten students seated at each table, with a teacher positioned at the head. There was no limit to the amount we could eat, but nothing must ever be left on our plates. And there was a hard and fast rule to be observed at all times: absolutely no talking during the meal. Saturday night was the cook's night off, and it was a night to be dreaded. The substitute chef was a teacher whose culinary talents, if he had any, had never manifested. The best he could manage was a huge pot of plain, boiled, burnt beans Saturday night after Saturday night. We all filled our hungry stomachs with Postum and bread until Sunday morning, when the cook returned.

It was good news and bad news when the regular cook retired. The good news was that the new cook fed us a breakfast of an orange, scrambled eggs, bacon, and toast, none of which we had ever had before. Lunch was the same: a table spread with all sorts of foods we had almost forgotten existed. We were elated. The bad news was that, by dinner, the new cook had been fired and we were back to burnt beans and watery Postum. A series of other chefs came and left. We were always hungry, the more so since we were working extra hard outdoors in the cold for hours at a time.

I guess since John's death I was always pretty much a loner. Even in boarding school I loved going off alone to the brook or up in the hills where I could watch for woodchucks and pheasants. Here at school, we couldn't leave the grounds without permission, and we had to have been well behaved for a long period of time before this permission would be given. One Saturday, after I'd been especially good for some time, I asked the principal if I could go to the pond. All hell broke loose. "You know very well our baseball team is playing this afternoon, and you don't even want to be there?" he shouted at me. "Where's your team spirit? You get yourself a rake and you rake every inch of the spectators' area and don't you dare stop until I tell you to. Maybe then you'll learn some team spirit. Get out of here and get to work!" he bellowed. I raked for the next four or five hours, but I never did manage to get any of that team spirit.

For a young boy like myself, who preferred and needed solitude, there were too many people, too many unpleasant and meaningless demands, and too little time to be alone at St. Bernard's. I was counting the days until graduation, knowing after that I would never return to this place again. Then, just a few days before graduation, something happened that rerouted my life completely.

We were all in the main study hall, where sixty desks were lined in four rows. My desk was in the farthest corner away from the pencil sharpener. The teacher sat in the back of the room on a raised platform. To get permission to sharpen our pencils, we had to raise our hand with the pencil in it and hold it there until the teacher looked up and gave a nod. On this particular evening, while one boy was sharpening his pencil, his friend waiting behind him jabbed him in the seat of his pants. The pencil went farther in than he'd anticipated, which sent his friend to his knees, screaming and rolling around. The jabber took three quick steps back and sat down in his chair as fast as he could.

The teacher on duty that night was new, and already none of us liked him. We resented his military attitude and his loud, harsh voice ordering us around. He jumped down, ran over to pull out the still-imbedded pencil, and hollered, "Who did this? Who did this?" His rage was building and his face was getting redder by the second.

Way in the back of the room someone called out, "Tepper." It was said in fun, since anyone could see there wasn't even a remote chance I could have done it and returned to my seat so quickly. Nevertheless, the teacher stomped across the room, stuck his face in mine, and shouted, "You're really in trouble now, young man." I didn't do it, I told him. I never even left my seat. "You did. I saw you!" he roared.

"You're a liar," I yelled back. The teacher was right. I was in big trouble now.

He was furious. He stared long and hard at me, turned on his heels, and headed back to his desk. But that was far from the end of it. The following morning the principal called the school together. He climbed up on the platform and announced, "We had a very serious incident here in this room last night. A teacher was called a liar in front of all the students. We cannot tolerate accusations and behavior like this. Tepper, stand up and apologize this instant or walk out of that door and never come back again."

And that's what I did. I got up, walked out that door, and never looked back. I walked all the way home to Millington. It was a long, hard, twenty-mile walk, and I only got a ride for about a mile of it. I walked in the door of our home and burst into tears. Fortunately, my parents believed me and were understanding. Despite the fact that I'd passed all my exams, I wasn't allowed to graduate from the eighth grade.

The highlight of that summer was a two-week camping trip on the Delaware River with my father, who was the local Boy Scout master, and his troop. One day on the camping trip, one of my friends and I got a boat ride four miles up the river and then swam the entire way back without stopping. Having seen this, the father of one of the scouts offered my father twenty dollars to teach his son to swim. With ten dollars of that money my father took me across the river, where he hired a pilot to take us up in a Curtis JN40, a Jennie with the OX5 engine. It was the first time in a plane for both of us, but it was the beginning of a love affair for me.

I spent the rest of that summer swimming and hiking with a few friends I'd made. The summer passed without incident, except for the time a gang of Italian boys came looking for trouble. I heard them yelling, and when I went to the edge of our property to see what was going on, I sure wish I'd stayed put. Some of them had tapsticks. These were three-foot-long pieces of wood, smooth and tapered on one end, with a thick piece of iron with a hole in the center taped and threaded. They were used on railroads for bolting things together. Boys would steal them, put one on the small end of a stick, hold the other end, and swing it over their heads. The tap, or nut, would sail out for several hundred feet. Just as I approached the gang, my parents called me to come in. Too late! I got slammed on the right side of my head. The blow knocked me down and cut quite a gash in my scalp. I missed my brother more than ever.

Chapter 2

Westering

I guess my folks could see how lonely and unhappy I had been ever since John's death. One night my father climbed the stairs, came into my bedroom, and said, "Son, if you had a choice, where would you like most to be living?"

It didn't take me long to answer that question. For months I'd been pouring over magazines with pictures of wild horses and cattle ranches in Oregon. I'd read about the homesteads being offered, and I'd dreamed day and night about what my life would be like if I only lived out West.

"Well, maybe it's time we begin to think about that," my father replied. I could hardly believe my ears.

But the subject didn't come up again until the following spring. Certainly, I hadn't given up dreaming of living in the West, but by then it seemed unlikely that it would ever come true. And then, out of the blue, my father asked if I had a particular place in Oregon in mind. I was prepared for that question. I showed him an ad for free homesteads still available in Sheridan and where to write if you were interested. The next thing I knew, my father was boarding a train heading for Oregon.

It seemed like forever before he returned. I lived in my imagination. I saw myself riding a coal-black, wild horse I'd roped on my own. I pictured myself rounding up stray cattle and sleeping out under the stars with only the coyotes and bears for company. In every frame I was alone in the wilderness braving the unfamiliar elements, happier than I'd ever been. When at long last my father returned, he brought pictures of the homestead land and tales of the friendly people he'd met along the way. I begged him to tell

Tom and their 1923 Ford Model T all set to head west to Oregon.

those stories over and over, and my fantasies became bigger and better with each telling.

It was settled. We would move to Oregon. My father and I began planning every detail of the move. The first thing he did was to put our place in Millington up for sale. Then he bought a 1923 Ford Model T with a small two-wheeled trailer with a hinged roof that was perfect for carrying our camping gear. Then together we carefully mapped out our entire route. We would follow the Lincoln Highway that went from the East. We'd go through Detroit, cross the Mississippi River somewhere near Davenport, Iowa, on through Nebraska near North Platte, on into Wyoming near Cheyenne, up to Boise, and then Napa, Oregon. I could already smell the clean air and the evergreens, and I could see myself with my first buck.

My mother was to stay behind until our new home was built. Who knows how she must have felt as we chugged out the lane that morning. I'm afraid I only knew how I felt. The ecstasy must have been radiating all over my face. Dreams really can come true.

My father kept a meticulous diary of our trip, and he wrote to my mother every day. Because the roads were all gravel, crushed rock, or just plain dirt, we averaged only nineteen miles an hour the entire trip.

Our biggest problem, though, was the soft, red rubber-type inner tubes in our tires that wore through so easily and constantly leaked. Every flat tire meant jacking up the wheel, removing it, and prying off the tire. Finding the hole was the easy part. After that, we'd have to put the 'Moco Monkey Grip' patch on it, let it dry for a few minutes, put the inner-tube back in the tire, and then put the tire back on the wheel. Then came the hard part—twenty minutes of pumping air back into the tire. Naturally, the tires always seemed to go just when we were crawling up a steep hill. Then my dad had an ingenious idea. We would pick up hitchhikers—big, strong, young men who were willing to show their appreciation for a ride. Well, he'd let them show their gratitude by helping us repair those troublesome tires. It worked beautifully.

There were no motels, hotels, or fancy bed and breakfasts, but there was no shortage of places to camp, usually by a creek or a river, until we reached Wyoming and Idaho, where camping areas grew fewer and farther between.

When I saw my first jackrabbit, I felt like I had just been welcomed to the West and to the beginning of the life I was meant to live. At a campsite in Green River, Wyoming, I was even made to feel like a hero. It was a hot afternoon and I'd hit the water the minute we'd settled in. I swam the distance across the wide river and crawled up to rest before swimming back. When I looked up, I was surprised to see a bank-to-bank mass of log sections floating down the river about a quarter of a mile away. If I headed back immediately, I felt sure I could beat the logs. I swam much of the way under water, which must have worried the fifteen or so concerned campers who'd gathered on the bank to watch me. As it turned out, they were impressed that I could swim at all, let alone swim cross the river and back. That was when my father and I learned that few people in sagebrush country ever learned to swim.

Near Ontario, Oregon, just across the Idaho line, our old Model T decided it had had about enough. We stopped at a garage, but the cost in time and money to repair the engine didn't suit our pocketbook or our schedule. We rattled along until we saw a ranch. Since cars were at a premium there, it wasn't difficult to talk the owners into trading a buckboard, two horses, and an eight-month-old colt for our tired old Model T.

I learned to drive the team pretty quickly. I may not have been riding the range yet, but I was definitely coming closer. The roads went from bad to worse, but the warm hospitality that greeted us along the way more than made up for that. Invariably, by late afternoon we'd pass a ranch and be invited in for a meal and often a night's lodging. Our horses were treated with the same welcome. Most of the ranchers saw so few people that they were starved for news from the outside and for conversation of any kind. Frequently, we had trouble breaking away in the morning.

By the time we reached Prineville, my father realized that at the pace we were going we would never get to Sheridan in time to file on the homestead. He needed to hop a train and get there quickly. That meant I would have to cross the rest of Oregon alone. We figured the smartest thing to do was some more trading. We swapped our buckboard for an old but stable riding saddle and a packsaddle. We also gave up the mare and her colt for a saddle horse and a young mare named Rosie. Since the other horse was also good for riding, we decided to keep it, too. My father gave me a few lessons in saddling the horses, drew a map for me to follow, and waved goodbye.

The freedom to ride the countryside cowboy style had come more quickly than I'd imagined and I wasn't about to complain. I was thirteen and the vast wilderness stretched before me full of adventure. I suffered no lack of confidence. I'd learned to cook en route, the horses were gentle, and I had a fine, clear map for directions. Early the next morning I eagerly set out on what had to be one of the most exciting days of my life. I felt independent, brave, and ready for whatever might come. It wasn't that I fought off bandits or rattlesnakes, or swam any wild, white water that first day that made it so memorable. It was the idea. I was alone. On a horse! In the West!

I spent two uneventful nights at ranches before reaching Sisters, the little town just under the three sharp, snow-covered peaks called Three Sisters. I put the horses in the livery stable and then went to see about a pass I'd need from the Forest Service before crossing the mountain. They refused to let me go alone. It was too easy to lose the road, they said, and I'd no doubt end up losing myself. They were sorry, but I'd just have to wait until someone came along who knew the way, and folks who crossed the top of the mountain were few and far between. And, no, they had no idea how long a wait I faced.

So much for my independence! Two days out and I was forced

to have a babysitter take me over the mountain. I might have to wait days, maybe even weeks, before anyone showed up. Besides, what if they didn't want my company?

Surely I had a guardian angel, though. Almost immediately word came that a young man was heading to Sweet Home to be married and he'd be crossing over the very next morning. And yes, he'd be willing to take me along. I was up and saddled before daybreak, raring to go. My companion-to-be came riding up on a beautiful, prancing, gray horse. Maybe the trip wasn't going to be so bad after all, I thought.

We reached the top at Elk Lake just before dark. There was a Forest Service building, a corral, a barn, and even a small pasture for our horses. The only problem was my guide must have planned to live on love. He'd brought no food whatsoever. When he saw my supply though, he decided rather quickly he couldn't live on love alone.

Everything was going so perfectly, that it wasn't until we woke in the morning to find our horses gone. Someone had left a gate open at the far end of the pasture. It took some time until we found all three horses happily standing in the middle of the shallow lake.

It was easy riding that day since it was all downhill. By early afternoon, the bridegroom decided I could make it on my own. "Just head toward the dynamite blasting and then follow that road to Sweet Home. You'll have no trouble," he assured me. And off he galloped toward his waiting bride.

That was fine with me. I was alone again and it was just as I'd imagined, even better. Patches of wild strawberries, and incredible beauty in every direction. By the time I reached the road, the work crew had already eaten. The cook took pity on me, though, and made me a good dinner before I headed on. It was almost dark when I spotted a small homestead with smoke pouring out of the chimney. What a welcome sight! It meant supper and maybe even a bed for the night. I knocked on the door, but instead of the warm welcome I'd expected, all I got was a man's head poking out of the door yelling, "Go away, git, git git on out of here." I had no choice but to git and ride on in the dark.

Luck was with me. I soon came across several men camping beside a car. They invited me to spend the night with them. I didn't refuse. It was a good place to stop. There was a creek and plenty of grass for my horses. The men were up and gone before daylight. It was the first day of deer season and they weren't about to waste a minute. While my horses grazed, I thought about my good fortune. Not long ago, I'd been back in New Jersey hemmed in by signs and houses and people. Now I was alone with my horses in the middle of God's mountains and forests, experiencing all the things I'd been aching to do. It was the blessed taste and sound of solitary freedom.

It took me four more days to get to Sheridan. Each night someone took me in and fed me, as well as my horses. One night, though, I was jolted awake from the cot where I was sleeping on a rancher's porch. The sounds of frightened, squawking chickens and ducks brought the owner tearing out the door, a .22 rifle in his hands. We could see several men running down the hill in the distance, but they quickly disappeared in the corn patch. My host pointed his rifle into the corn patch and fired again and again, shot after shot, until we heard a painful shout, "Stop, I've been hit." The rancher beamed as he lowered his gun. "Now we'll catch those thieves for sure 'cause he's gonna have to see a doctor," he said, grinning from ear to ear. Apparently, several men had been raiding local chicken houses and rabbit farms, and no one had been able to catch them. I left the next morning, so I never heard the end of that story.

My father's map made it easy for me to find our new homestead. By the time I arrived, my father had already laid out a cabin with the help of an old homesteader living nearby.

Chapter 3

The Zenith: Oregon

Building the cabin was every bit as much fun as I had pictured. My father and the old homesteader had already felled a number of small trees, so in no time the three of us had the walls up, the rafters cut for the roof, and a sixteen-inch-long wheel cut to split into shakes for roof shingles. We found a stove and stovepipe in an abandoned homestead.

Besides our helper, there was only one other homesteader in the vicinity, about a mile away. It was also a mile walk to the mailbox. Deer were plentiful, but the brushy country made it difficult to hunt. I explored every inch surrounding our place. In the south corner was a virgin-growth Douglas fir forest, with trees from four to seven feet around. Once inside those firs, it was almost impossible to see anything but the sky above. An easy place to get lost in, I decided.

Only two things could have made me happier than I was: to have my brother with me to share my new life, and to have my own deer rifle. On October 15, 1924, the day I turned fourteen, one of my wishes came true. A brand new Winchester .30-.30 caliber carbine arrived in the mail, a gift from my cousin Sim. It was the perfect deer rifle for hunting in that area. I got my first of many bucks that year. Through the years I have taken such tender, loving care of that rifle that it's still in mint condition in the hands of my son John.

It didn't take us long to learn the reason for so many abandoned homesteads around. It began to rain, and it rained and rained for eighteen straight days. Secondly, though the land was free, there was no way to earn a living, so many had to leave just to survive. My father had to leave for a different reason. He was having trouble breathing at that altitude. His near-fatal pneumonia and his battle with typhoid fever had left their marks. He had no choice but to go down to Sheridan to live.

Again, I was left on my own. I spent most of my time hiking, chopping wood and occasionally helping out the old homesteader, who'd lend me magazines to help pass the long, cold, rainy winter nights. I especially looked forward to the staple groceries my father would send up with the mailman.

In April I rounded up Rosie, took my rifle and a few belongings, and rode down to join my father in Sheridan. He was living in a small hotel and keeping books for many of the local businesses. My mother was still back east trying to sell our house, so we moved to a ranch outside of town and became caretakers there. Ellery, the ranch owner, was a small-time dealer in livestock. He'd buy his horses from Eastern Oregon all 'broke' and gentle, and bring them to the valley to sell. Seems no one in the valley wanted a horse that wasn't gentle. One horse no one wanted to buy was a small four-year-old filly. She moved okay, but with her long neck and back, and short legs, she wasn't much to look at. Ellery and my father made a deal: they'd trade Rosie, who was neither a saddle horse nor a light work horse, for that filly. Because I was given the filly on Easter Sunday, the filly was henceforth known as Easter.

When at last our house in New Jersey was sold, my mother and grandfather sent their belongings by railroad in a boxcar and took a train to their new home in the West. Finally our family was reunited. My father bought a Model T and we set about the business of finding a home for all of us. We settled on a lovely small farm two miles from Willamina, about eight miles west of Sheridan. Our two-story house was by a creek, and the land had almost every kind of fruit and nut trees that could grow in Oregon. I could reach out of my second-floor bedroom window and pick Royal Anne and black Bing cherries.

I got my first job loading and unloading firewood, cleaning stalls, and feeding horses for a Mr. Fox, the owner of the local livery stable. I also exercised Fox's eighteen-year-old, two-thousand-pound, pure white Percheron stallion he'd bought from France. No cinch or girth was large enough to go around the Percheron, so I would ride him bareback down the main street of town with only a halter and a small chain around his lower jaw. It was like riding a steam engine. If another horse came along, I'd find the nearest pole as fast as I could and tie him up, otherwise the Percheron would charge, and there I'd be. Once, I made a big mistake and let him gallop. And gallop we did, until he finally decided he'd had enough. I'd had enough long before, but he wasn't going to quit because some small, scrawny little kid thought he should. But it was another horse I fell in love with—a horse left in the stable by a man who said he'd be in the pool hall if anyone needed him. I took one look at that horse and knew I had to have him. It was a small sorrel gelding, the best looking horse I'd ever seen. I didn't waste a second. I ran over to the pool hall, waited impatiently until the men finished the hand they were playing, excused myself and said "I want to buy your horse." He leaned back, lit up a cigarette, and said, "Thirty dollars." Now, that was a lot of money when all I got was an occasional fifty cents, but I asked for directions to his place and left. I was determined to have that horse.

There was a four- or five-man sawmill up above our farm and I'd heard they were short one man. I applied for the job and was hired on the spot by the boss, a man called "Slab-tongue Charlie." A name well suited. He was the most abusive, foul-mouthed person I'd ever met. He never did an ounce of work himself, and since he didn't dare cross the other four men for fear they'd quit, I bore the brunt of his mouth. None of the locals would work for him, but I needed the dollar a day he was paying me, so I hung in. I stashed those paper dollars in an empty snuff can and counted the days until I had my thirty dollars.

One day, Charlie ordered me to carry a heavy, thirty-inch-round circular saw down a steep trail to the road. I knew it was way too heavy for me, but there was no reasoning with Slab-Tongue. I did fall and cut my hands and leg pretty bad. Charlie just laughed. I wanted to quit right then and there, but I also wanted that horse. It was worth anything I had to go through.

I went through many such days before I had my sweet revenge. One morning Charlie took me to a new site, handed me a pick and shovel, marked a six-by-ten area where the steam engine would be placed and told me to dig down about two feet. Charlie climbed back in his car and rumbled off, leaving me alone. I picked and shoveled the whole day and rode Easter back the next day to finish the job. When Charlie arrived, he scowled and swore at me for not finishing the job in one day. I was dripping with sweat, but I kept quiet and just kept digging. At the end of the day I collected my dollar and rode out for the last time, brimming with satisfaction. I had my thirty dollars and no intention of telling Charlie I wouldn't be back. I knew the other men weren't about to do pick and shovel work, and it would be days before Charlie found someone who would.

The next day I grabbed my snuff can and rode Easter out to collect my sorrel. I rode right into a moonshine operation run by the sorrel's owner and three other men. I pretended I had no idea what was going on. I just handed the can to the man. "Never use the stuff," he told me. "Look inside," I told him. He counted out the dollars, and without a word more led me out to the pasture.

There he was, as magnificent as ever. I put a halter and rope on him and rode him home. I named him Ginger. It fit both his color and his personality perfectly. The only saddle I had was the old one we'd gotten in Prineville on our way west. My Ginger deserved better. I chose a beautiful one from the Hamley Saddle Company in Pendleton, Oregon. I've had some wonderful horses, but none were ever as good as Ginger. We had something between us. He just seemed to know what I wanted without being told. I only let one other person ride him and that was only once. Ginger let him stay on a short distance, and then he plopped down. I got him up, my friend got back on, and Ginger plopped down again. We tried it several more times, with the same results.

The next job I took was as a whistle punk for a high-lead logging outfit up on the hills west of our farm. The outfit's job was to get the large trees down from the steep mountains to the sawmill. There were no track-laying caterpillar tractors then, so they put a large steam or diesel engine on the top of a high ridge over the trees to be cut down. The engine furnished the power to pull a cable, wound around a spool, up and down the steep slope with a tree-length log attached to another log. The cable went around a pulley (sheave) at the bottom, which was fastened to a stump. The man at the top was called the donkey puncher. The man at the bottom was the hook tender.

My job as a whistle punk meant that I was moved around on the top of the steep incline to where I could hear shouts from the hook tender below. I'd transmit the hook tender's hoots into signals and send them to the donkey puncher. The engine was extremely noisy. One whoop from the hook tender meant go ahead. If it was already going ahead, it meant to stop. Two whoops meant go ahead slowly, three meant back up, and four meant back up slowly. It was a simple job, but it carried a lot of responsibility. The hook tender could get badly hurt or even killed if I sent the wrong signals. Don Mendenhall, the donkey puncher, and Truman McNutt, the hook tender, had been partners for a long time. Without a whistle punk, Don had to walk out about a hundred feet to the edge to be able to hear Truman a quarter of a mile below. I saved them a great deal of time by standing on the edge and relaying the signals.

There were two other workers: a man with a team of draft horses and a man who spent the entire day sawing the tree lengths into eighteen-foot pieces with a one-man crosscut saw. The teamster would pull out a log from under the spar tree and take it to where it would be sawed. He'd then drag the lengths a few hundred feet to the other side of the ridge where the men and I were. There the logs would be rolled into a chute in which they'd slide about a mile and a half down the mountain. From there they were loaded onto trucks and taken to the mill.

One day I had an opportunity to watch the old, grey-haired, bearded man who felled the trees for them. For safety it should have been a two-man job, but this old man couldn't get along with anyone, so he'd figured a way to pull the eight-foot crosscut saw by himself. The saws were so thin, they couldn't be pushed, only pulled. I was amazed to see the rig he'd designed. He was using a rubberman—long strips of rubber from inner tubes braided together. He'd fasten one end to a tree and the other end to the end of his saw so that it would pull the saw back. With that, he was felling all of the three- or four-foot- round trees we were pulling down.

At the time, I was riding a three-year-old filly named Lucy to work. She was a gentle horse owned by someone who just wanted her ridden more. I would ride her up in the morning, remove the saddle, and tie her up in the shed behind the barn where the team-ster kept his horses. At quitting time, Lucy wasted no time running on the trail through the timber for the mile up to the ridge where I would have to open and shut a gate before going on.

Though it was after sundown, it was still light enough to see when we quit work one evening. I saddled Lucy, but her bridle wasn't where I'd hung it on a spike. I was furious, especially since I'd just put a pair of new leather reins on it. I'd seen a couple of men near the barn earlier that day, but I'd figured they were the men who greased the chute. Guess I'd figured wrong. I had no choice but to take a turn around Lucy's lower jaw with the halter rope and hope I could control her with that. We started off down the grassy slope. All went well for a couple hundred yards until the trail made a sharp turn to the left into the big timber. At this point Lucy must have remembered home with a passion. She broke into a dead run and there was no way of controlling her. I saw the trees looming ahead with only darkness between them. I was scared to death.

Waking up was like coming out of a bad dream. My head felt like a jackhammer was pounding on it, and my forehead was swol-len and bleeding badly. It was so dark that the only things I could see were the stars above. And then, slowly, it all began coming back. But where was Lucy? I got up and stumbled down the trail. When I got to the gate, there was my father holding a lantern in one hand and Lucy in the other. She had a big lump over her left eye and a piece of leather was scraped off my new saddle. I was angry enough to want to kill her. Thanks to my father's calming influence, that didn't happen.

The next morning I rigged up another bridle and went to work. On the way, I saw exactly where Lucy had failed to make the sharp turn and where we'd crashed into a large old Douglas fir tree, but I never did find out who stole my bridle.

I worked with that outfit until they ran out of logs and had to move to a new site near Grand Ronde. The men picked me up to take me to the new site until the rains began. With the mud almost waist-deep at the spar tree, and me with no rain gear or boots, regretfully I had to quit.

It wasn't long before I found more work. It was a simple job with poor pay, but I needed it. I was in no position to be particular.

All I had to do was open gates for a truck driver in Willamina who was hauling cants from a mill up in the hills. My agility came in handy. Our route went up through three ranches, each with a cattle gate across the road. The road was so steep in places that the driver would have to put the truck in low gear. I would jump off, run ahead, and open the gate. When the truck was through, I'd close the gate, and run to catch up and jump back on the truck.

Once the sixteen-foot-long, foot-wide cants were loaded, we'd repeat the procedure going back down the hill, with me sitting atop the cants. The driver was a small man, but strong. He had to be. He had to unload those cants at the railroad siding by himself. He was grateful to have my help, though it was only for a few weeks.

My next job was more to my liking. I signed on as a general hand for Jim Savage, owner of a large ranch several miles south of Willamina. Each year Savage drove his steers over to the coast, where his daughter and her husband owned a ranch near where the Salmon River flows into the ocean. He'd turn them out there to graze on the grassy capes overlooking the ocean. The grass grew fast and so did the cattle. They got so fat they had trouble walking. In the fall we would ride back to the ranch to drive the steers home. We'd spend one night, then turn around early the next morning to drive the fattened cattle home. Because they could make only a little over four miles a day, the return trip took a week.

It was on our way back with the cattle that I saw something I'd never seen before. There were only dirt roads then, but the road crews were cutting a strip through the forest to start the new highway. They felled the trees and then sawed them up into twenty-foot lengths on the large end and up to forty feet nearer the top. They used an auger to drill holes a foot or more deep and pounded in wedges full of black powder. The wedges had ten feet of heavy iron chains fastened to them. We watched a man put a short fuse in the end wedge, light it, and walk away. The log blew into pieces. The horses dragged those pieces over to piles, where they were left for a year to dry before being burned. It was a terrible waste of good wood, but there was no way to drag it out to where the log trucks could pick it up.

I learned a lot working for Savage. I watched traveling crews shear goats for their valuable mohair and sheep for their wool. I learned to trim their hooves. If the animals had been kept on soft, grassy fields for too long, the hooves often got so long they could hardly walk.

I watched pigs being butchered, and I learned how best to smoke the meat. They used an airtight building eight-feet square with a small door on one side. The ceiling was twenty feet high and had pulleys fastened to it and ropes for pulling up the sides of ham and bacon. In the center of the dirt floor was a circle of flat rocks for the fire on which each morning it was my job to build a small fire with a bundle of dried willow and alders. This sent a column of smoke to the top where the meat was hanging. The building was so tight I could usually see a haze from the previous day's smoke. It was a job well worth the trouble. We were fed generous amounts of either ham or bacon every day.

I liked my work and my boss, but it was in eastern Oregon, where the largest ranches were, that I really wanted to be. The next summer, when I was seventeen, I decided to try my luck there. I'd heard it wouldn't be easy, but I knew by now that miracles happen. I sold a couple of my horses, but I kept my precious Ginger, since my parents agreed to take care of him. I bought a used Model T Ford Roadster, sent a dollar and a quarter to Salem for a license, and a few days later received it in the mail. On the back was printed, "This license is permanent unless revoked." No driving test! Nothing!

My father offered to ride with me the first day. I threw my saddle and gear into the car, and we set off down the old Highway 99. It was mostly gravel and very narrow, with only a few pull-outs for passing. When we drove into Grants Pass, we were astonished to see the tan faces on the children. We were so used to the grey-white faces of the Willamina children who looked up into constant clouds and fog instead of the sun. What struck me most about that trip, though, was the sight before our eyes as we crested the hill and looked out over the entire Rogue Valley and the Pitt, which is now called Mt. McLoughlin. There it was in all its glory, covered with snow. Never had we seen a sight so lovely.

It was almost dark when we reached Medford. We rented a room for the night, and in the morning my father caught a bus home. I headed up the old Green Springs Highway to Klamath

Falls, then turned toward Lakeview. When I stopped for gas in a small town, I asked a man dressed in work clothes if he knew where I could find a job.

"Sure," he said. "I just quit one. You can probably have that if you want it. The job's okay, but the boss is a dirty so- and- so."

To get a job so quickly was indeed a stroke of luck, but working for a dirty so- and- so wasn't exactly what I'd had in mind. I took the job, which was to be spring farming—putting in oats and rye. But first, I was told by the boss, I was to feed the horses each morning. That was fine with me. I took the oats into the first stall and then innocently went on into the second stall. I'd no sooner entered, when the large bay there gave me a swift kick with both hind feet, knocking the can out of my hands and almost taking my fingers with it.

"Yeah, that horse will do it every time. I forgot to warn you," my new boss said, laughing. That was just the first of several incidences that day. I already understood why the man before me had quit.

When Sunday rolled around, the young cook asked me to drive her to her fiancé's place fifteen miles away up in Langel Valley. Everett, her boyfriend, was out working cattle, but his parents were home. She showed me Everett's silver-mounted bridle and spurs, his good Frontier Model Colt .45 revolver, and his handsome saddle horses in the meadow. I was sure impressed. Then his parents asked if I'd like to help them prepare their fields to plant oats since Everett wouldn't be back in time to help. I agreed to help them, but only after I finished the planting I'd already promised to do.

When Everett returned, the two of us rode over the mountain and down to Clear Lake, where he showed me wild bunches of horses. He pointed to several that belonged to him, and offered to trade two for my Model T. That was just fine with me. I chose a well-built brown gelding and a sorrel with a blaze. I preferred the sorrel, but he was running with a fast group and we couldn't get close to him. We managed to corral the brown gelding, and I worked with him four or five days before he tamed down enough so I could ride him.

Then it was time to look for more work.

Chapter 4

Buckarooing Bonanza

It was a stroke of luck that I was asked to help drive several heads of stray cattle over the mountain. On my return I was on the road to Malin in the Tule Lake area, most of which is in California, when a stranger asked where I was heading. The man was Bill Dalton, owner of four large ranches in the area. He offered me a job on the spot.

We rode on together to the home ranch, where thousands of tons of hay were mowed and stacked each year. That's where I would start—with the haying. All the haying was done with horse-drawn machinery. It was cut, raked, and piled into stacks sixteen feet wide, a hundred feet long, and eighteen-feet high, and shaped like a bread loaf. A wooden slide was pulled up and the hay was piled on rope nets spread on the ground. Several draft horses would then pull the nets full of hay up the slide. A couple of men on top of the stack stopped the nets and opened them when they reached the right position. A long rope was fastened to the end of the nets. That's where my job came in, and I needed a good saddle horse for my part of the operation. I would wrap the other end of the rope around the saddle horn several times, and then gallop away to pull the nets back down to the bottom of the slide. This went on from daylight until almost dark, with only an hour off for dinner. At least we were always well fed.

By the third of July, the hay was stacked and the entire crew moved up to the Steele Swamp Ranch, twenty miles east of the lava beds, and we started all over again. Over a thousand head of cattle were spread out over at least a thousand acres of natural meadow, with several ice-cold springs. There was no bunkhouse for the men, and, since there was no shortage of mosquitoes in the meadow, we were forced to retreat to the lava beds for sleep. There we arranged and rearranged rocks, piled hay on top of our lumpy 'mattress,' and tried to settle our aching bones in between what felt like miniature mountains.

It was there that I was given the name "Skeeter Bill," because, they said, I looked just like old man Skeeter Bill Robinson, who used to work there. And because, they said, I was so tall and skinny that I could stand in the hot sun and only a faint shadow would show up after a few minutes. That name followed me all over cow country for many years.

One evening just at dark a Forest Service truck pulled in and commandeered several of us to fight a fire that was out of control on Pine Mountain southeast of where we were. After being bounced down the road several miles to connect with other fire crews, we were each given a shovel and told to pick up a can of food from the table. Someone would bring us water, we were told, before we were whisked off and ordered to continue making a trail around the mountain. It was miserable, slow, hard work—so smoky we could barely breathe, and so dark we could barely see where we were, let alone where we were going. Neither of us had watches, but we figured it'd been at least three hours and no one had brought us water. We finally stopped to open one of our two unlabeled cans with a pocketknife. Corned beef hash! The last thing we needed when our mouths were so dry we couldn't even spit. We opened the second can. More of the same! We left them on the rock and went back to work. It was morning before someone came, not with water, but to tell us the fire was under control and we could go on down to the main camp for breakfast. What a useless exercise we'd been put through, except that on the way back we found a baby wildcat crouched under a log. My partner wrapped it in his jacket and carried it down to where fifty other worn-out fire fighters were eating a breakfast cooked by a man hovering over a large wood stove. The cook admired the kitten and offered us a dollar for it. Sold!

Sixteen years later that same chef was cutting my hair in a barbershop in California. Of course it took some random 'conversationing' before the truth fell out about how he'd been a cook in Modoc County working for the Forest Service fighting fires. And yes, he'd raised the kitten to full size. When it got to be too much trouble to keep, he gave it to the Bakersfield Zoo, where it was a favorite for years.

Once we got the hay in at the Steele Swamp Ranch, I figured I was out of a job again. Just as I was leaving, though, Pete Milton, the buckaroo boss, asked if I'd replace the young man who'd been riding with him, as he'd just quit. Would I ever! He had me turn in the horse I was riding, and in its place he brought me Sandy, a large, grey, excellent saddle horse. I'd be buckarooing at last, and not just in my dreams. Driving cattle was much more to my liking than haying, that's for sure.

The cattle were spread out for miles, some across the line into Oregon. Most of our riding was on the lava beds, where millions of years ago a sheet of molten lava rock several feet thick was spread out over that entire part of the country. Eventually the ground below settled and the sheet of rock cracked into millions of small pieces. Grass grew up in the cracks, and it was this grass that was so nutritious for the horses and cattle.

Horses raised on those lava beds could walk, trot, or run across the rocks easily and almost never fell. But a horse ridden across the rocks had to be shod with iron shoes, and those wore out every couple of weeks. In a day's ride, a horse wouldn't have all four feet on the ground at the same time for more than a few hundred feet. Well, someone had to shoe those horses, and since there was no ranch blacksmith around, each rider had to shoe his own string of horses. Each man had six to ten horses in his string, each horse weighing up to twelve hundred pounds. Holding up the weight of a horse's hind leg was no easy job for someone as skinny as I was. A horse can transfer much of his weight from one front leg to the other, but the entire hind leg is a different story. We needed both hands and arms free to use the rasp and to hold and drive in the nails at exactly the right angles. When the nail comes out an inch or two below the shoe, it has to be cut off or bent over immediately, because if the horse jerks its leg, the nail could easily stab our leg. The scars on the inside of my upper legs are proof of how frequently this happened..

We rode seven days a week from daylight to late afternoon, with no lunch. Then we shod a horse or two, ate supper, and hit the hay. And there was always the odd experience, like the time we rode over to another Dalton Ranch about twenty miles away and met Tuck Courtwright, the caretaker. He invited me to ride with him in his Model T to get some ice. A few minutes later I was most sorry I'd accepted. I watched him go berserk just because as he was cranking his car it kicked back and hit his arm. He grabbed the crank, pulled it out, and used it to beat the radiator and hood with all the might he had available. He had a pretty good set of lungs, too, along with a 'sailor's tongue.'

Milton, who was standing next to me in the barn, grabbed my arm, pulled me outside, and we ran like crazy to get out of Tuck's way. Two minutes later, out came Tuck, running around like a wild man. We watched from afar until he seemed to have himself under control, then we gingerly crept back to the barn. There he was, all ready to go, so I had no choice but to grab some courage and climb in with the man. Later Milton told me Tuck had these fits of uncontrollable rage periodically and that's why he has to live alone. In fact, he knew himself well enough that he put his guns in padlocked trunks in the house and he put the keys to the trunk upstairs in the barn so he'd need a ladder to get to them. He figured by the time he rounded everything up, he'd be of clear mind and wouldn't be likely to kill someone.

On my one day off that season I rode over to Willow Creek, where I'd seen an old Indian fire ring, and where the famous Captain Jack surrendered. I found dozens of perfect arrowheads and at least a dozen brass buckles from U.S. Cavalry bridles. It was a wonderful day made even more special by the hundreds of mule deer, sage hens, and assorted bird life I saw.

Branding the calves was the next order of business. Two ropers took turns roping a calf and dragging it to the fire where the branding iron was heated. My job was to push the calf over, grab his tail, sit down, and put one of his feet into the crotch of the hind leg and hold the tail tight. One man cut the ears while another did the branding. A third man castrated it if it was a bull. With two ropers we could do about two hundred calves a day. At first I was kicked all over, usually onto some awful, smelly, slippery ground. Eventually I learned how to avoid being kicked, but I never learned how to stay clean. Later I worked on ranches where the ropers were so good, they roped the calf by both hind legs. All I had to do was sit down, get the tail and leg, and take the rope off. Not only was it easier, I never got kicked.

Before any of us did any branding, we were given a serious lecture about caring for cuts and scratches while we were in the corral. If cut, we were to lick it, suck it, spit it out, and keep on working, because dry horse manure on the ground could easily cause gas gangrene. There was no sulfa or penicillin to take care of it then. The only cure was amputation. We were told that our own saliva was the best antiseptic and that air would help the healing, therefore we should never bandage a wound tightly.

September and October we were busy rounding up and bringing in the cattle. About that time I got a letter from my parents saying they'd sold the Willamina house and had built a new house in Ashland, Oregon. They had a surprise waiting for me there. By early November the cattle were in and I was free to go to Ashland. Nothing could have made me happier: There was my beloved Ginger out in a pasture. My parents had even built a small barn for him.

I fell in love with the area immediately. It was so different from the country in eastern Oregon and northern California. There were so many trees and shrubs I'd never seen before. The Mount Ashland watershed was only a mile or so behind our place, and I spent hours walking the trails and exploring the abandoned gold mines. I stayed in Ashland for the winter, but by April I knew if I wanted to find work riding again, I'd have to go back to the Daltons'. I bought a Model T with the money I saved from my summer wages, and said goodbye to my parents.

This time luck was not with me. Pete Milton had died and Dalton didn't need me. There were no other jobs, so in desperation I took a short-time job working with a couple of old-country Irishmen helping to lamb out about three thousand ewes. Eventually they moved the entire flock close to Clear Lake, where my sorrel colt was still running. This time I managed to corral the sorrel. I named him Chacho. Using the same tactics I used with the brown gelding, I was soon riding him.

Once the lambing was done, I had to look for work again. The only problem was that one of the Irishmen had borrowed my car and bent the fender badly. We made a deal much to my liking. I'd never told the Irishman what I'd paid for the car, and since cars were a lot less expensive where I bought it in the Rogue Valley than they were here, I sold it for the price I'd originally paid. With that, Chacho and I took off for Modoc County.

En route we stopped to spend the night with the infamous Tuck Courtwright. Tuck seemed to be in control of himself and was even letting a railroad crew use part of his house for cooking and eating. They were building the railroad from Klamath Falls to Alturas, and the right-of-way went right past the barns and canals.

I left the next day in time to reach the Black's Canyon Ranch before dark. I was hoping to see Jerry Stratton, the buckaroo boss, about a job. I'd met him on several occasions the summer before. Stratton was away, but as was the custom, Tom Ivory, the ranch manager, invited me to spend the night. When Ivory realized I had ridden in on a green colt, he was impressed and asked if I'd stay and ride a couple of horses that needed attention. The oldest and truest saying about turning a wild colt into a gentle saddle or work horse is: You have to have more time to spend than the horse. I had the time, and Ivory had two good-sized, four-year-old, black geldings for me.

It's an easy procedure. I began by spending hours rubbing their backs with an old gunnysack and picking up their feet. By the third day I could ease a saddle on them and lead them around. By the fourth day I could get on and off and ease them around the corral. By the sixth day I rode them outside the corral and back, and a week later I could ride them anywhere.

I lost that job because of an efficiency expert who'd arrived unexpectedly and questioned the need for paying me when Stratton was perfectly capable of training the horses. Ivory tried in vain to get in touch with Stratton, certain that he wouldn't let me go. When that failed, Chacho and I were forced to leave. We headed for Alturas.

Luck had found me again. The stable keeper there knew that a man named Charlie Demmick ran a large ranch nearby, that he was in town, and that he was looking for some help. Obviously, Demmick was careful whom he hired. He spent fifteen minutes checking Chacho for saddle sores and looking over my bridle and saddle before he told me to ride on over to the home ranch at Likely. The ranch was the largest in the area, turning out nearly five thousand head every spring. This was big time, and I was excited.

Earl, one of the ranch hands, told me how I came by the job. A few days before, Bing Wah, the ranch cook, gave the buckaroos fresh steaks for dinner. Since they all knew there had been no butchering for weeks, they asked Bing where he'd gotten the fresh meat. Bing told them that one of the cows had gotten on her back in the ditch and couldn't get up and he couldn't get her up. She died within about ten minutes because the weight of her innards kept her lungs from working. So, rather than waste the meat, he'd gone back for a sharp knife and some pans and cut off as much meat as he could reach. To him it was the logical thing to do, as the cow was reasonably fat and the meat should be edible. The men thought differently. In fact, the idea repulsed them.

The boss drove to the nearest phone, called Charlie Demmick, and said they'd all quit if he didn't fire Bing Wah. Charlie asked why on earth he should do that. "Because he was trying to get us to eat meat from a dead cow," the boss yelled. "Well, you wouldn't want to eat her alive, would you?" Charlie yelled back. To which the boss responded, "We quit." And they did. And that's how I came to get the best buckarooing job I ever had.

I was working on the home ranch of the "Big Four," an old Miller and Lux Ranch, sixteen miles along the south fork of the Pitt River. Sure it was long and hard work, but I wouldn't have traded my job for any other on earth. Where else could I have seen such breathtaking views as when I rode over the high Warner Mountains? From the top of Cedar Pass I could see halfway across Nevada. I vowed then that I would never take nature's beauty for granted.

Charlie often paired me with a young Indian named Eddie Hess to work with some of the young horses and some of the rough string. Once a horse has been mistreated, he seldom gets completely over it. It takes a lot of patience and care to erase their bad memories enough so that they can be ridden without bucking. Eddie and I were a good team.

Eddie didn't talk much. He could ride all day and not say a word. I remember the day we were taking some cows to a ranch about twenty miles away. Several men in a car stopped and asked Eddie if he knew where someone named Jones lived. Eddie just shook his head. The man stomped back to the car, saying purposely loud, "That dumb injin don't know nothing."

I was shocked when Eddie told me about the incident. Even more so when he said, "I wonder what the man would have to say if he knew I graduated from college." It was the first I'd heard that myself. Indeed, he had gone to school in Likely and earned such good grades he was given a scholarship to a college in Sacramento. Though he had a degree, as an American Indian the only work he could find were the traditional jobs open to any other Indian. He came back to the same work his father'd had when Miller and Lux owned the ranch. Eddie wasn't even allowed to enter a restaurant or a barbershop unless he was with white buckaroos.

One of the worst experiences I had during my buckarooing days was the time we were riding out with our new buckaroo boss, a man none of us could stand. He could only ride gentle horses, which didn't give us too much to admire about him either. Along with the boss, Austin McCrary, a new buckaroo, and I were moving some seventy head of cows and calves to a ranch two day's drive to the west. It was a hot July day and we knew there would be no water until we reached a pond in late afternoon. What we didn't know was that the pond would be so dry there wasn't even any mud. The cattle were thirsty and restless.

The next morning we started out at daybreak hoping to find a spring Austin remembered. It was off the trail, but we were desperate. The cattle were getting out of hand, and it was still a long way to our destination. It wasn't worth the detour. All we found was mud. It was a hundred degrees and there was no shade along the way. Since we had no idea if any of the ponds had water, when we saw a ranch in the distance, we were desperate enough to head for it. But distances are deceiving, and it took until four the next afternoon to reach that ranch.

Being so dry that your tongue is swollen all the way from the back to the front has got to be the worst pain there is. I swear, you would kill your own mother for a drink. That's not the case with lack of food. I've gone without food, and I just got uncomfortable and weak, but without water, something happens to your brain. You lose reason and morality.

We rushed to open the ranch gates to let the cows in, and we headed for the ranch house sheltered under some cottonwood trees. Only we didn't get that far. A dirty pond came first. Austin and I saw that pond, fell off our horses, and gulped that water as fast as we could. It didn't even bother us that it was covered with green scum or that we were drinking right along side our thirsty horses. There was no way we could have waited until we got to the house.

There were other days when I wished I could have gotten in a position to kick myself. Like the day Eddie and I were moving a small bunch of cattle up to a ranch near Alturas. We were on the main dirt road running from Alturas to Reno. There was very little traffic then, but at one point we had to move the cattle over to let a Model T pass. The driver stopped and motioned for me to come over. "I have to get to Reno," he said, "but I'm about out of money. I'll sell you my watch for ten dollars." It was a good Hamilton watch with a six-inch chain made of what he said were gold nuggets. It was called a railroad watch, since it was the kind engineers used to keep time. I showed him all the money I had: two dollars and some change. He took it. I was sure he'd cheated me, but for the life of me I couldn't figure out how. That night I showed it to the buckaroos. When Earl offered me five dollars, I stupidly took it, figuring the nuggets were probably only brass. That Saturday night Earl went to Alturas and returned laughing. He'd taken the watch to the jeweler and gotten twenty-five dollars for just one of the nuggets. I suppose the watch had been stolen, otherwise the man would have taken it to the jeweler himself.

Austin and I had reason to think we might lose our jobs on one of our trips. They sent us up to a small leased ranch east of the Madeline, where riders had picked up twenty of our steers and put them in their pasture. We spent the night in a cabin, and the next morning set out to take the steers to the railroad in Ravendale, where Charlie was to meet us. It promised to be an easy ride. Austin had a tall, gentle, buckskin horse and I was riding a colt. We were only about a mile out, when one of the steers stopped, looked around wildly, and charged a juniper tree. He butted and bawled, and white slobber was flowing out of his mouth. Then he fell down and just lay there. Five minutes later he was dead. We were beside ourselves. Surely, Charlie would think we'd run him to death, which can happen with an overweight steer. If so, he'd fire us immediately. After another mile or so, the same thing happened to another steer. Then we remembered the rumors that there were rabid animals in the vicinity. A rancher had been bitten by his best gentle horse. The horse died soon after and the man was taking rabies shots.

Austin told me he'd heard that a cow could survive if you drew blood from him by cutting off his tail close to his body. I was crazy to believe such a wild tale, but I was willing to try anything. I held Austin's horse while Austin took his sharp pocketknife, walked over to the steer, lifted his tail, and pulled the knife up through the tail. That steer was back on his feet in a flash, charging Austin, who was by now in a dead run for his horse. His horse was gentle, but he'd never had anyone run straight at him, especially on his right side. (Horses are always mounted on the left side.) That poor horse whirled around right in front of my colt, and, of course, my colt then whirled around too. Austin's eyes were huge with fright. Somehow he'd managed to drop his knife. It was a wild circus for a few seconds. Fortunately, the steer fell over and died before he got to Austin. By the end of the day, we'd lost fourteen more. We were worried sick.

Luckily, Charlie had heard the same rumors and believed our story. In fact, by the time we got back to the ranch, one of the men, Henry Fitshugh, was taking rabies shots. He'd gotten off his horse to pull up a loose wire on a fence and hadn't seen the sick, emaciated coyote lying in the tumbleweeds until it bit him on the hand. Henry trampled the coyote to death and brought it back to have it confirmed for rabies.

When the riding was over that year, I asked Charlie if I could quit to go see my parents and whether I would still have my job the next spring. "You can have your job here for the rest of your life if you keep on working as well as you have," he assured me. That was high praise coming from him, and it certainly made me feel good. Unlike the other men who took their pay each month, I had Charlie save mine in a bank in Alturas, all except for a dollar or two. When I collected my pay, it was mostly in five and ten dollar bills. (Twenty-dollar bills were seldom seen in those days.)

I caught a bus home, and in the morning when my father asked how I'd done I proudly pulled out my roll of bills. The only money I'd spent was for a few sacks of Bull Durham tobacco for ten cents each. "Don't ever carry that much money on you. Someone could hold you up and you could get hurt. Put that in the bank," my father said. When I told him I had saved that money for a new Chevrolet roadster, he agreed to go with me to the Chevy dealer in Ashland so I could buy it immediately. Unfortunately, they were out of the model I wanted and wouldn't have more until the next month. At my father's insistence, we went directly to the bank and deposited all but a dollar seventy-five. That was Thursday, October 28, 1929.

The next day is one I'll never forget. My father went to his office as usual, but soon he was back, his face drawn and strange. "The banks have closed down all over the entire country," he said. As soon as he'd heard it on the radio, he'd gone to the bank and found the doors solidly locked. Black Friday. My father never forgave himself for making me put the money in the bank. I lost it all. In 1950 I got a check for fourteen dollars as my share of the bank's assets. I'd put in over six hundred.

I'd brought my saddle to Ashland so I could still work, but no one had money to pay me. I could always work for board and lodging, but still I'd need clothes, boots, and shoes. I managed to kill a couple of small black-tailed bucks. It was illegal, but most of the time law enforcers looked the other way during those hard times. A local blacksmith and I worked a deal. I rasped the hooves and held the horses while he nailed on the shoes. He could work twice as fast, and we split the pay. Prices were going down everywhere. Gasoline was ten cents a gallon, and a quarter would buy a good meal, pie and coffee included.

As soon as it was spring, I took a bus back to Alturas and looked up Charlie. He drove me out to the meadow and showed me about two thousand beef steers. "Look at them," he said, "They should have been shipped out and turned into beef by now. I haven't been able to sell a single one. I've had to let all my hired hands go. There's no one left here but the Indian."

So there would be no working for Charlie that season. He knew of a ranch where I could at least stay and sweat, which meant work for food and lodging, but no wage. I rode Chacho, who had spent the winter at Charlie's, over to the ranch. I lasted there only a few weeks. They had me sleeping in an old shed, and the no-good, lazy son-in-law of the owner gave me the worst jobs of all, though one of them eventually led to a strange experience.

The son-in-law belonged to the American Legion, which had given him an assignment, which he, in turn, passed on to me. The story was that some ninety years before, when the West was still unsettled, General Crook and his troops pursued a group of Indians into the rocky cliffs with large caves under them. When Crook's advance party came in front of the caves, the Indians killed many of the soldiers. Now the local American Legion was upset that none of the graves had ever been visited. So on this Memorial Day he was to take a bunch of little American flags and place them on the graves. The problem was neither of us had any idea where the caverns were, only that they were somewhere in one of the four mountains across from there.

I took one of the colts and set out on this odd task. I found nothing on the first two mountains, but on the third I could see in the distance what looked like caves. It was too steep to ride up, so I tied the colt to a tree and climbed up. There it was. No fence, just enough rocks piled around it to make the graves visible. Most of the markers had fallen down, but because the air was so dry, they were still fairly readable. Most of the names were Irish. I put up the flags and crosses as best I could, and then went up to look in the caves. Nothing there.

It was on the way down that I passed an old homestead where a couple of old men lived. I knew one of them, an old-country Englishman who'd lived in Alturas for a long time. He was a happy, well-liked drunk. When they saw me, they came running out yelling for help. They were in a real fix. One of the cows feeding in the area had fallen down their drinking well. The well was about sixteen feet deep, but the water level was only five feet deep. They had an old car and an odd plan. "How 'bout if we let you down on a rope and you tie the rope around the cow. We'll use the car to pull her out. Then we'll let another rope down to pull you out with," one of them suggested, obviously pleased with his own idea.

I wasn't pleased. I didn't think much of the plan, but I didn't think much of leaving the poor heifer down the well either, so I agreed. When I got to the bottom, I found myself in a soupy, muddy mess where the cow had been furiously pawing. This well was only about three feet around, not much room for both of us, and the miserable cow was bent in a circle. Once they let the rope down, I tied it around her short horns. Both men were peering down at me while I stood in this slop counting the seconds until they'd pull me out. Minutes went by, and then suddenly the rope around the heifer tightened—and up she went in a hurry, shedding slime all over me. I knew that if the rope broke, I was a goner.

In the meantime I could hear the men laughing and having a good old time up there. At least five minutes passed before one of them finally called down, "Are you okay, lad?" What a question! I was fit to be tied. They lowered the rope, and hand over hand I climbed up out of that hole. The heifer hadn't been at all happy about her predicament either, and she was letting them know it. The more she kicked about, the more the men teased her. As for me, rather than dirty my saddle with my filthy clothes, I walked the quarter of a mile to the Pitt River and washed them there. The sun was going down by then, so I had to wear them wet back to the ranch.

The next day I packed my things and left. I rode over to see Tom Ivory's brother, Ed, who managed the ranch west of Alturas. He wanted me to work, but he couldn't offer much pay. Anything was better than my last job. Ed was a good man to work for. He had some unusual ideas, but they seemed to work. For example, all the riding and draft horses had to have bits in their mouths. It's unnatural to them, and it's hard to get them to open their mouths for the bit. Ed's solution was to keep a few pints of whiskey bottles filled with syrup throughout the barn to slop on the bit. The horses loved the taste and soon learned to drop their mouths down and take the bit.

While we were taking several hundred head of cattle up to the lava beds to the old Avazina Capura Ranch, I saw something I'd heard of but had never seen for myself. We had the cows and calves mixed together. A couple of cows had given birth that day. Before sundown we stopped them in a large, flat area and the cows went in search of their calves. I noticed that one of them hadn't yet found her calf. "Watch her," Hank, one of the steady riders, said. "You wait. She'll go back to where she last saw her calf and the calf will go back to the same spot too." We headed back to where the calf had been born. Sure enough, there was the calf tottering in that direction too. We followed it. When it got to the place, it lay down. Not much later, sure enough, here came the cow. "Even if the calf was a month old, the two of them would return to the same spot if they were separated," Hank said.

It's too bad a mare and her colt don't have the same instincts. If they're out of hearing distance, they can't find each other. That's one of the reasons I quit running wild horses. There might be hundreds of colts running, trying to keep up with the mares. Their hooves wear down quickly and we'd find them dying of thirst, their little hooves all bloody.

It took us three days to get those cattle to their summer range. I'd been to that ranch before, when I rode from Steele Swamp. That evening the caretaker, Jack Davis, showed me some beautiful conchos and a lovely silver-mounted bridle he had. Then, from his possible bag (a bag that holds socks, razors, etc., usually carried with the bedroll) he took out a good-looking razor strop. He had me hold it, look it over carefully, and then tell him what kind of leather I thought it was made from. It was light colored with fine grain, nice and pliable. I guessed and guessed, but never came close. It was human skin! From his friend! It was true. He showed me an article from a Reno newspaper from about thirty years before. Jack and his friend were working out of Reno then. His friend got in a fight with a man and shot him to death. He was sentenced to hang, but before he died he gave a university permission to dissect his body. They skinned his back to see what kind of leather it would make. Jack asked for a piece of that skin, and since this was his best friend, he had it made into this strop. Had I had a million years, I never would have guessed correctly.

Not long after that, we were taking some horses to the Avazina Ranch to work cattle. Charlie, a sixteen-year-old lad who came from a poor family with a drunk for a father, joined us. Just as I had been, he was eager to learn all he could about riding. He'd never ridden anything but gentle old plugs, so he was given a nice, well-bred, brown colt to ride. Both Hank and I had ridden him a number of times. He never bucked and had no bad manners. He was just a little skittish and restless.

Before we left I read there was to be a total eclipse of the sun on April 20 beginning around ten or eleven in the morning. I told Hank and we decided to have some fun with Charlie. As planned, just when the sun seemed to be darkening, Hank turned to me and asked if I'd heard anything about the world blowing up that day. With a straight face, I assured him I had indeed. The sky was getting darker and darker. Suddenly, Hank jumped off his horse and tied him to a juniper tree. With great drama, he threw himself on the ground, covered his face with his hands, and began pleading to be allowed to live a little longer. He begged forgiveness for all the awful things he'd done. I followed suit, only laid it on even more. I apologized for killing innocent people and groaned about being so ashamed since it was only for a few measly dollars. We had ourselves laughing so hard we didn't dare show our faces.

Meanwhile, poor Charlie never got off his horse, and by then his horse was really prancing and dancing all over creation. It had grown so dark we couldn't see more than a hundred feet. The eclipse lasted about twenty minutes. By then Hank and I had confessed to at least fifteen murders, several bank robberies, and who knows what else. We didn't say a word. We just climbed back on our horses and rode off.

Charlie came tearing up behind us. "Why did it get dark?" was all he dared ask. "It was just a warning this time, I guess," I told him. "If we don't change our ways, it'll get us the next time for sure." The farther we rode, the harder we laughed, until eventually we had to tell him the truth.

Hank and I went deer hunting together once. Only once. Hank was riding a gentle, but high-spirited buckskin. At first we only saw does and fawns, but then suddenly there was a yearling directly in front of us. Hank jumped off his horse, and holding the reins with his right hand, raised the rifle and shot. His poor horse had never heard a bang like that before. He jerked the reins loose and took off in a dead run. Hank levered in a new cartridge in seconds and fired at his horse, who by then was at least two hundred yards away. I whipped my horse around and headed for the buckskin. Hank was already levering in still another cartridge when I caught his horse and brought it back. "Why in the hell did you shoot at your horse?" I asked. "I didn't want to lose my saddle," Hank answered. I was livid, but I didn't argue. It would have served no purpose.

Poor Charlie got it again from us. The youngest and newest always goes through an initiation period it seems. Though this time he deserved what he got. Each evening when we'd get back to the ranch, we all had to pitch in to get the chores done. There was water to fetch, firewood to be readied for the stove, and cooking to do. Charlie's job was to drag the large juniper limbs back to the ranch on horseback and then chop them with an axe. He was a good man really, except for one thing: he always disappeared when it was time to do his chores. Hank and I ended up doing them night after night. We never knew where he disappeared to until we found him sleeping on a sofa in a room with no windows. We were irritated enough and devilish enough to devise a plan to end this nonsense. He slept soundly, so it wasn't hard to do. We flooded the floor with a couple of pails of water and put a couple more nearby. Then we tied one end of a short rope around one of Charlie's ankle, and the other end to the sofa leg. It was just long enough to reach from the sofa to just past the flooded area. We spread a bunch of newspapers over the water and then set fire to them. We ran out of the room and closed the door except for an inch or two so we could watch. With both doors to the room almost shut, it was pitch black. We yelled, "The house is on fire!" Charlie sat bolt up. We threw open the door and Charlie tried to run toward us. When he reached the papers and tried to jump over, the rope caught him and down he went. We threw a pail of water on him. "You sons of bitches!" he yelled when he saw what had dropped him to the floor. Believe me, after that he did his own chores.

It wasn't too long after that when bad news arrived. There were no cattle or horse sales, so no revenue. Ed was told to let some hired hands go. I was one of the lucky ones. I'd heard that a buckaroo on the Gerber Ranch up north had quit and his job was open. I saddled up Chacho and rode due north over the hills to Clear Lake, right through the area where Chacho was born and raised. I spent the night at the Steele Swamp Ranch and reached the Gerber Ranch the following evening. I got the job, but it meant working under Sikes, the foreman.

Sikes should have been mending fences. Despite the high opinion he had of himself, he wasn't much of a cowman, let alone a foreman. The first morning he showed me a large gelding, a fairly good-looking, bald-faced bay. He said that when the gelding was three, a ranch hand tried to break him, but was bucked off. Several times they put him in harness alongside a gentle horse and tried to work him hard to tame him. Nothing seemed to work. He continued to buck everyone off. Now it was my time to try.

I knew it wasn't going to be easy. Obviously, he'd had nothing but rough treatment and pain from humans, and I didn't look much different to him. I put my saddle on him, got on, and got exactly what I expected. The bay hung his head and tried his best to get rid of me. One horse will buck high and hard, landing on all four feet so forcefully that the rider is seriously jarred, yet it's not hard to stay on. Another horse will make one high jump and twist in the air. "Go up toward the east and come down in the west," as the saying goes. It's much harder to stay on a horse that does that. Lucky for me, this bay was the first sort. I rode around the corral easy until he caught his breath, then I got off and stroked him with my hand.

I asked Sikes whether this bay was to be one of my string. "That bay *is* your string," he said. I needed the job badly, or I'd have left right then and there. Instead, I said I'd give it a try as long as he let me train the bay my way. Several times a day I rode him around the corral, and while he didn't get gentle, at least he got used to me.

Then came the day Sikes told me they were short a ranch hand and I had to help out. So instead of riding, I'd be pulling out a grove of willow trees. They were using teams of horses to pull the scraper to fill the holes once the trees were out. My job was to handle the scraper by means of a long, iron handle behind it. I had no shoes, only my riding boots, which were certainly not made for walking in all day. That evening I went along with the others to the pool hall. I'd never learned to play pool or cards, so I just watched. Eventually I got bored enough to try the slot machines. I put my coin in, pulled the lever, and out tumbled quarters all over the floor. My little dime had won me several months' wages.

According to Sikes, no new ranch hand showed up the next day either, so I'd have to be on the end of the iron handle again. It was then that one of the buckaroos told me Sikes had told them all that I was so afraid of the bay that he'd have to make me a ranch hand. That did it! Sikes was nowhere in sight, so I saddled the bay and rode out with the buckaroos all day. When Sikes found out the next morning, he handed me a few dollars and said he was letting me go. That suited me just fine. I told him exactly what I thought of him and added that I was taking that bay with me. Someday I'll bring him back, I told him, but right now I have no intention of leaving him behind.

That bay gave me the ride of my life on the way back to Ashland, though. Chacho's back was ripped badly by a nail in the abandoned, old barn we stayed in on the Green Springs that night. I knew since I had no corral to start the bay from that he would be almost impossible to ride, but I had no choice. We were twenty-five miles from the nearest corral. It wasn't light yet when I eased myself up on the bay. He bucked, whirled around, and took off galloping through the thick timber. I thoroughly expected one of my legs to be scraped off on a tree. The bay crossed the creek in two leaps and then started up through more timber on the other side. The slope slowed him down. When he finally stopped, I got off, rubbed his neck, then got back on and rode him back to Chacho. He never bucked after that.

Chapter 5

Ranch Life, Horses and the Depression

That March I heard that George Noble might be needing an extra hand. It took Chacho and me four long, miserable days to reach the Nobles'. We were riding in freezing rain, and winds so strong they blew some roofs off in Klamath Falls, about ten miles east of where we were struggling along. Luckily, I'd stopped in Midland and bought a ten-cent can of sardines and a five-cent pack of crackers. I survived on that until I reached Noble's.

Noble agreed to use me to help gather a bunch of wild horses, but it was understood there would be no money involved until we caught and sold the horses. By this time there was a market for horse meat, and Noble intended to sell the horses to the Schlesser Brothers Canneries in California and Portland. I agreed. After all, I had to eat. Harry Charley, a half- Hoopa and half- Klamath Indian, showed up about the same time. George knew him from when he rode with a man named Lester Hickson, so he took him on, too. Our first job was to bring in the horses. Next, there would be cattle to bring in and brand, and haying to be done at the Pre-emption Ranch.

Again we were faced with the problem of trying to sleep while the mosquitoes were trying to eat us. Fortunately for me, Harry and I were bunkmates; he'd been all through this before. The first thing we did was to look for some large juniper fence posts and a few short pieces of rope. We made a ladder with poles we found and then carried the posts up on top of the barn and laid one on each side of the gable, about two and a half feet down. We tied them together with ropes on each end, took fresh hay and filled it level over the gable to the posts. We put our bedding over that and enjoyed a restful, undisturbed night. Not a single mosquito climbed that high for its dinner.

Harry had also figured out a way to have cool water all day long—a much-desired comfort when we were stacking hay in the heat of the day. Since our elevation was at five or six thousand feet, it was often close to freezing at night. We'd fill our two-gallon canvas water bags at the spring each night rather than in the morning and then hang them in the shade where they'd stay cool until mid-afternoon.

After haying season, it was back to running horses. George gave me a roan for my string, a roan that bucked every time he was ridden. George had watched the way I'd won over a mistreated horse named Gray Dog, so he was convinced I could handle the roan. I thought I could. The roan's habit was to buck in a straight line until he ran out of breath. I worked with him for a while, until I figured the roan had gotten bucking out of his system. I was gravely mistaken. It didn't take long before I found out just how mistaken I was. I dismounted to open a gate to lead the roan through, climbed back in the saddle and rode on a bit before stopping to roll a cigarette. I got the paper out, held it in my left hand, curved it with my right hand to put the Bull Durham in, and in a flash I was airborne. I landed on my bottom with one half of the cigarette paper in each hand. The roan was well on his way back to the gate.

A few days after that, with no warning, the roan went end over end, sending me sailing down the steep side of the mountain. Other than scraped and bleeding hands, I was okay, but darned if the same thing didn't happen again soon after. The roan was running well, trying to get ahead of the wild horses, and suddenly he turned a somersault at full speed. I only had the wind knocked out of me, but his front leg was broken. "Just leave him," Harry said. "He has the spring to drink from and plenty of grass to eat. His leg will heal. I've seen this before." So that's what we did. We were just outside the Gerber Ranch when this happened, twelve miles from our ranch, with two riders, two saddles, and only one horse. It didn't please me, but I had no choice but to ask Sikes to borrow a horse. Common courtesy required that he lend me one, though it was the last thing he wanted to do.

I saw that roan again when we took another bunch of horses to the same area. His leg had healed, though he had a slight limp. Unfortunately, he was taken along with the chicken horses (the ones that were shipped away for horsemeat).

I had my share of accidents that summer. George had been given a spooky four-year-old sorrel that, as George said, tried to climb up my back as I led him out of the barn one morning. One of his front hooves struck me on the neck at the base of my skull. The other hoof hit me just above the belt in the small of my back. "He rode you all the way to the ground and then bucked again and ran across the corral, where he stopped and stood snorting," George told me after I woke up sometime in the night. That ended my riding for a number of days.

I'll never forget the day I met Lester Hixon. When I was finally able to ride again, George and I were moving cattle on a dusty road, when a new Ford Roadster approached. We pushed the cattle off to let the car pass, but instead, the car stopped and the driver hopped out. He was sporting a new suit, white shirt, and shoes shiny enough to see your face in. I'd heard plenty about Lester. Most folks in the area had. At fourteen he already had a fine collection of saddle horses and saddles—all stolen. He kept the horses up on a small meadow east of Hyatt Lake. Then his cache was discovered by deer hunters, who turned him in to the frustrated sheriff who hadn't been able to solve the case of the disappearing horses. Lester did a turn in reform school. When he got out, he came to George Noble looking for work. George had a feeling he'd be a good worker, and it was obvious he loved horses.

Stealing horses from the wealthy was a temptation Lester couldn't resist. He had a partner, Harry Charley, a friend of mine. Though Harry never stood trial, Lester was convicted a number of times for horse theft, and his last conviction was for assault with a deadly weapon. It was his fourth trip to the Oregon State Penitentiary, and he got fifty years. By now the warden and Lester were well acquainted. In fact, he'd grown rather fond of Lester and thought he had potential. According to Lester, the warden presented an idea to the parole board: They could make Lester a salesman. The state penitentiary raised flax that they processed into linen and linen threads. Some of these were woven into excellent fishing nets, but not enough people knew about them. If anyone could sell those nets, it was Lester. He convinced the parole board, and so here was Lester, all outfitted in new clothes, running around in a new car full of fishing net samples, and a good salary to boot.

I would have thought that would change Lester. No. It didn't take long for him to smell the sagebrush again. He drove back to the prison and told the warden he needed some time off. He voluntarily gave up his salary, returned the car, and hightailed it back to Klamath County to ride wild horses on the Klamath Reservation. Regardless of his faults, Lester had to be the most charismatic person I'd ever met. He was tall, dark, handsome, and very intelligent. Every now and then he'd show up at George's. On one of his visits I asked him about a bridle bit he'd given to George. It was made of stainless metal and beautifully carved. He'd made it in prison, he told me. I was especially interested in how he'd engraved it. I'd been practicing engraving on silver dimes on the Velvet and Prince Albert tobacco cans, the pocket size ones with red paint or finish on them. I'd gotten fairly good at it, and the designs came easy to me. He'd learned from his cellmate, he said. It had been the man's trade before he was sent to jail for engraving plates and turning out twenty-dollar bills. He'd been given a long sentence, but because he was a model prisoner he was allowed some engraving tools in his cell to engrave things for his friends. It was even possible then for the prisoners to buy a new watch, have it engraved and initialed, and give it as a gift to a family member. With a piece of copper, Lester showed me how to wriggle cut. I was hooked. It was a whole new adventure for me, and I was thrilled.

My friend Harry Charley has his own wild tales to tell. Harry and his friend, who was also an Indian, had gone to the Hoopa country not far from Eureka, California, where they knew they could get jobs in the sawmills. They were both in their twenties and eager to meet girls. With the money they earned, they bought new suits, shirts, and shoes for dancing. Saturday night came, but their hopes were dashed in a hurry. They could see white men dancing with Indian girls, yet the doorman refused to let them in. They moved on to another dance hall, but the same thing happened. This time they weren't about to accept a refusal. The police arrived in short order and they were hauled off and thrown in jail for sixty days for disturbing the peace.

No way were they going to stay in jail for that long. They became model prisoners. They ate their food, regardless of how bad it was, and they exercised daily. They still had their new clothes and shoes, and they had a foolproof plan. Thirty days later, they were ready. When the jailer brought them their evening meal, they grabbed him, locked him up, and out they went. They knew there would be a manhunt, but that didn't worry them because they were going to be going through a hundred miles of rugged mountains where it would be almost impossible to see them.

It's a hundred and ninety miles on a straight line from Eureka to Chiloquin, and at least twice that going by way of the mountains. When I asked Harry about that trip, he said the worst part was walking in those new oxford shoes. To keep their shoes softened, they had to wade in water whenever they could, otherwise they'd surely have blisters. By the time they got to Chiloquin, their shoes were worn to nothing. When I asked what they did for food, he said they had learned as children how to identify edible vegetation and how to catch and kill animals. The first time they even came close to other people was when they came off the Siskiyou Mountains near Talent, Oregon. It was around midnight when they came to a small ranch off the highway. There were milk cows in the field, and Harry and his friend squirted milk into their mouths until they had their fill, and then they filled an empty bottle they found by the road before continuing on to Chiloquin. Once they reached their destination, they knew they were safe among their own people.

When we were no longer riding out at the first daylight, I got to watch George's wife, Nova, milk Herefords. Now, this is a beef breed of cattle. They're not milkers. Not that Herefords aren't ever milked or that I hadn't seen cows milked before. This was different. These were semi-wild cows and their calves that George would bring in off the range for Nova. To take a range cow with her new three- or four- day-old calf and put her in a small corral and get in with her is asking for trouble. She'll charge you with her horn, intent on killing, and she'll hit like a speeding runaway truck. Nova's method was ingenious. She'd put on a large, floppy hat and a long dress hanging about two inches above the ground. Then she'd sing

Tom on his favorite horse, Ginger, taken in Ashland, Oregon.

a soft, persistent, peculiar sort of chant as she climbed up on the high pole fence. There she'd sit for a few minutes. Slowly, still singing, she'd start down on the inside. When she got down to about three feet from the ground, sure enough, the cow charged. Nora always managed to get out of the way, but the cow hit the poles so hard, the entire side of the fence shook. She and the cow would do this again and again until the cow finally decided it was a boring game and Nova could play it by herself. When she was ready to let Nova approach her, Nova would leave a small wooden box of grain near the cow. Nova would wait about an hour, and then return and turn the cows out to graze, or if it was winter, to hay. She repeated this for three or four days. It was startling to see the calf sucking on the left side and Nova milking on the right side a few days after that. She did this nine months out of the year. Occasionally, a cow would charge after she'd been tamed. Nova simply swished her big skirt out to the side, just like a bull fighter with his cape.

That Thanksgiving, while crossing over the Green Springs to get to Ashland, where I'd spend the winter with my parents, I met a man who invited me for coffee in a makeshift camp he was sharing with three other men. This was in the bottom of the depression, and these men had lost their jobs as carpenters in the Los Angeles area. Families with a man in the house were not eligible for help, so these men left their homes to ensure aid for their wives and children. Between them they had money only for gas and ten pounds of dry rice when they left.

I told them I'd worked on many ranches and yet I'd never seen a carpenter on the land. There were lots of houses and barns in need of repair, and surely since they'd brought their tools they could trade labor for food. I warned them against going to the cities for work. There were too many out-of-work sawmill employees hanging around. I also told them, despite the law, they could kill a deer for food. Lawmen were still looking the other way. In the high country they could easily make jerky with the meat since the air is so dry.

During that winter in Ashland, my interest in working with silver became an obsession. My father introduced me to a jeweler who willingly taught me all he could about engraving and silver soldering with a blowpipe and an alcohol lamp. He also gave me a catalogue that included everything I'd need to get started in a serious way. A week later I had two books from England and all the tools I'd need.

I worked day and night using copper to practice with, since it was similar to silver both in engraving and shaping, but considerably less expensive. I wanted to copy the superior silver work of the Spaniards—the beautiful silver ornaments they'd been decorating their horses' tack with for centuries. I was especially interested in making conchos, the small circular silver discs domed in the center. They were usually engraved, sometimes with the owner's initials, and were used to embellish bridle bits or the bridle itself. Because of the Depression, I knew there would be no market for them, but they could always be used for bartering.

Around this time the Depression was showing signs of improving. I think "Old Frankie D." did some foolish things, like killing newborn pigs to raise the price of pork, or dumping thousands of gallons of milk to raise the price of milk. No one had the money to buy any anyway, and there were no jobs. In my opinion, he finally did something that worked: he repealed the Eighteenth

Amendment to the Constitution, making beer, wine, and whiskey legal again. Thousands of farmers were allowed to grow barley for beer, corn and rye for whiskey, and grapes for wine making. Carpenters were needed to build breweries, and banks lent money to farmers for construction projects. This caused an instant reaction. After that, the recovery was in full speed.

Chapter 6

Post-Depression

George Chamberton, a good friend of mine who lived near my parents, was an outstanding violin player. He practiced each evening with his mother, a retired concert pianist from British Columbia. I loved classical music, and every night I could I invited myself over to listen. I loved classical music then, and still do. When George was asked to play at the Chautauqua building in Ashland, he invited me to come. The only problem was I didn't have the twenty-five cents to enter. No way was I going to miss it though, so I sat by the partway-open backdoor. There was one performer in particular I could have listened to all evening. He was one of the youngest, but surely the best. His name was Yehudi Menhuin. Little did I imagine that forty years later that same boy would be playing a violin made from my wood.

Toward the end of the Depression I was fortunate in finding work buying saddle and work horses for a ranch owned by Denver Parks and his family on the Green Springs at Jenny Creek. If I could have owned any ranch I'd ever ridden from, this would have been it. Jenny Creek ran right through the middle of the ranch. They had a large hay meadow, a big barn, good corrals, and just the climate I love the most. The ranch was situated so that it was open to the south and west, and under a huge rim rock. At night it dipped below freezing, and frequently the snow would be four or five feet deep, yet by eight in the morning the sun was up and we could shed our coats while we worked horses in the corral.

A man named Springsteen also worked on the ranch with us, though only on a daily basis as needed. He homesteaded forty acres above the ranch, where he raised potatoes to sell to his neighbors. One afternoon after a day of riding with Denver, I headed for

Ashland. Soon Dr. Haines passed me, speeding toward Ashland himself. I could see he had a passenger slumped over in the front seat of the car, and I thought it sure looked like Springsteen. It was.

Denver told me that after he'd left me, he passed the Miller Ranch and heard Mrs. Miller screaming. He rode over, dismounted, and ran up on the porch. Just as he reached the open door, Springsteen charged out the door and hit Denver in the face, knocking him right back down the steps. Since Mrs. Miller was still inside yelling, he had no choice but to get up and try to go in again. This time he was able to tackle Springsteen, but it took both of them to subdue this poor, crazed man shouting that he was the reincarnation of Jesus Christ. As soon as they managed to tie him up in a makeshift straitjacket, they called the operator to send the doctor. No one ever knew what made him go berserk. He'd always been a good, quiet neighbor.

Doc Haines was a big man with a big sense of humor. I was a skinny man with an innocent ear. When I saw the doctor a few days after the incident, I asked what had happened to old Springsteen. "Oh, this happens to a lot of older men who live in the woods. They get to eating too many baking powder biscuits and it drives them nuts after awhile." I believed him. I wouldn't touch baking power biscuits for years, even though they were the mainstay of backwoods and cow camp meals. I might never have eaten them again, but eventually I had an injury that sent me to Doc Haines. I asked him how come this baking powder was allowed to be sold without a warning when it's so dangerous. He near died laughing, and told everyone he knew about it afterward.

Springsteen ended up in the mental care state hospital. I got a letter from him some time later asking me to buy his homestead for a hundred and fifty dollars. I rode up, looked it over, and decided against it. It was a beautiful place, with two creeks, a small meadow, and lots of good pine and fir timber, but there was a high rim rock on three sides and no way of making a road into it with the equipment available then. I let it go. About fifteen years later, I heard it sold for eleven thousand dollars. The timber alone was worth that. I missed a number of similar opportunities, but at the time I just wasn't ready to be tied down.

I had an almost new .45 caliber Colt semi-automatic pistol

that Denver fell in love with. I agreed to sell it to him. He carried that pistol in a holster everywhere he went. The only problem with a semi-automatic is that when it's loaded and you shoot it, it ejects the empty cartridge and reloads a new one in the chamber. If you pull the trigger again, it will shoot and reload again, as long as cartridges remain in the clip or unless you manually let the hammer down and push on the safety. None of that was good news for Denver. He was riding a good horse I'd broken for him, when his dog ran a bobcat up a tree. Denver shot the bobcat, but it scared the wits out of his horse. It whirled around to the left, making for a dangerous situation, since they were on a fairly steep hillside. Denver, still holding the pistol, tried to grab the right bridle rein. He caught the rein, but unfortunately touched the trigger by mistake at the same time. The pistol fired again. The bullet hit the horse in the back of head and killed him instantly. He dropped down, pinning Denver's leg under him. The pistol had fallen out of his hand when he hit the ground, and when the horse got through his death struggle, as Denver said, "The damn pistol was lying there a couple of feet away, reloaded and aimed right at me." It took him some time to dig himself out. You can be sure that's the last time he ever carried that pistol.

The next work I found was with a couple from Medford who were starting a riding academy at a ranch on Cottonwood Creek above Hilt. It was my job to find and break the horses for them. Working for them provided wild and occasionally dangerous experiences, but none of it was as hard work as my next undertaking.

Chapter 7

Cattle Guarding

Hugh Baron, a local rancher I knew, asked me to work for the Keene Creek Cattleman's Association for the summer. They ran about two thousand head of cattle on the area from the Green Springs Highway on the south to Dead Indian on the north. On the west side, the Forest Service boundary was across the top of the mountain from the Green Springs summit to the Dead Indian summit. My assignment was to keep the cattle off the Forest Service land until the first of June, or until the snow was gone and the grass on the meadows on top was high enough that the cattle wouldn't tramp it down into the mud. Cattle had ruined too many meadows in the past, so the Forest Service was impounding any cattle found over the boundary. They required the owner to pay twelve and a half dollars a piece to get them back. That was half the value of the cow back then, and a calf was the same penalty fee as a cow. I received the princely salary of twenty-five dollars a month, plus I had to furnish my own horses and horseshoes, as well as food. It was a tough way to get rich, but I needed the money to provide more tools for my silversmithing.

On the thirty-first of March I was set. I had a packhorse and good saddle horses. They'd already begun putting out over seventeen hundred head of cattle down around Emigrant Lake, where the grass was already green. Up where I'd be staying, there were still about two feet of snow. My cabin was small, but it had a good wood stove for cooking and heat.

I had little to do until the first of May. By then the snow was gone from the valley and most of the hillsides, and the cattle had grazed their way up to about the three-quarter mark of the mountain. Mostly it rained, and the snow was melting fast down on the slopes. Each day the cattle would move closer and closer, and each day I'd have to chase more and more of them back down. The situation grew steadily worse. The cattle had eaten most of the grass, and they were hungry and determined to get to the top, where they knew there was plenty of grass. I was counting the days until June first and wondering how long I could continue to put in such long, strenuous hours. I had to borrow an alarm clock from the dam keeper nearby so that I could awake before daylight, which was when the older cows began moving. I rode every day until it was full dark, changing my horse three times a day.

Was I ever relieved when the last day of May arrived! Much to my sorrow though, Hugh arrived to tell me that the June first date had been canceled and the cattle were to be kept off until the Forest Service gave the word. Most of the meadows on top were still snow-covered; it had been an unusually harsh winter.

The next two and a half weeks were the hardest I've ever put in. My horses and I were exhausted. The cattle were all bunched together trying to get across, and it took me almost twenty-four hours a day to hold them back. By now I was setting my alarm clock for four in the morning. I had to put an old, tin washbasin over it to make it louder. The busiest and hardest times were between four and five in the morning, and again just before dark. I discovered that the only control I had was to drive the worst bunches as far as possible back down the mountain, since it took a long time for them to climb back up. But this was hard on the horses. I was existing in a sort of daze. When a member of the association finally gave me the good news that not a single cow had been impounded and I was free to let them go, I was too exhausted to celebrate. I just nodded and said I had to get some sleep.

The hardest part of the work was over. My job now was to put salt out for the cattle. Range cattle need plenty of salt, and it needs to be put in the same place every year so they learn where to find it. The coarse salt, crushed like fine gravel, arrived in fifty-pound bags. The salt was put out in logs, hewn by hand, into a trough with both ends closed. I fashioned two of these myself—a three-day job done with a dull axe. After all that, the logs never lasted long. When it rained, some of the salt dissolved and the brine soaked into the soft wood. Too often, other creatures chewed the wood to get the salt.

Porcupines were the worst offenders. They could eat holes completely through the trough. The advantage of the logs is that many cows can get to the salt at the same time. Salt bricks last longer, but only one cow at a time can enjoy the salt. That means they spend more time fighting than licking. In the past the men had dragged the logs into a clearing, but then the cattle had tramped down the grass around it. In an attempt to improve the range, they'd ordered all salt sites to be moved into the timber areas. This made sense, but it angered the older ranchers because they had trouble finding the new sites.

It was late afternoon and drizzling when I finished putting the salt out one day. I was riding a bay on an old trail on Tom Spring Mountain. Suddenly, for no reason, the bay gave one quick jump to the left, just as though a gun had been fired in its right ear. It wasn't until much later that I awoke. It was pitch black and pouring rain. There I was, lying on my back in the mud, gagging and choking, and oh was my head pounding. I rolled over on my side and spit out something big and slimy. The entire left side of my face hurt and was badly swollen. I had no idea what had happened. I managed to get to my feet and stagger down the trail. It wasn't until I saw fresh horse tracks filled with water that I remembered my horse. Then it all came back to me. I had to walk the rest of the way back. The bay had found its own way back.

I returned the next day to see if I could figure out what had happened. There was the imprint where I'd fallen in the mud, and there beside it was a red object that looked like a piece of raw liver. I realized it was a piece of clotted blood. And there was the fir tree that had had its lower limbs sawed off years before. A three-inch stub of a limb was left, and on it was a piece of my skin. The bay had always had a habit of unexpectedly jumping to the left, but I'd always been lucky before. Guess I was lucky this time, too. Had the bay been four inches taller, that stub would have punched out my left eye. I never rode that bay again. I couldn't afford to; I lived too far from anyone for help.

Once the salt was out and the cattle were spread out, I was ready to move up to my summer camp near the northeast corner of the lake. At one time, the Barrons owned all the land around the lake. There was a large meadow with springs up at the north end, a house, a barn, and plenty of land for growing hay. Since then a company has bought the land, built the dam, and taken the water down to irrigate around Ashland. There used to be a small lot and a house at the north end above the water line. The house was used occasionally for hunting and fishing, but I was given the keys in case I needed to get in. I was to stay in a homesteader's cabin a half-mile away and another quarter of a mile up from the lake. I'd have to walk back and forth. (Why is it we say back and forth? How can you go back to something until you have gone forth? Rightfully, it should be forth and back.)

I loaded my scanty belongings—a frying pan, a couple of pots, coffee pot, dishes and a bedroll—on the packhorse and rode up to Hyatt. I'd never been there before, and I was eager for adventure. I had no problem until I started up the north side. Though it was the fourth of July, the snow was still breast-high on the horses. The worst part was the crust on top. The poor horses had to jump and then plow to get through it. It took them a long time just to cover a hundred feet. When I saw blood and realized both horses had cuts on their front legs, I turned around and went back to the ranch for the night. The next day the sun was melting the snow rapidly, so I broke trail for the horses, and we finally made it up there.

Near the cabin was a fairly new car. The paint was still good, but right in the middle of the car was a large dead Douglas fir snag that had fallen on it. I was told that the homesteader who owned this place had come from Los Angeles. He'd made the road into his place from the Barron Ranch and built the cabin himself. He was afraid that big snag might fall and crush his car, but he hadn't the foggiest idea how to take such a monster down. He asked around and was told to put in an undercut and then make the back cut. Simple. He bought a short one-man saw and set to work. The undercut alone took several days. When he felt he was ready to let the tree fall, he moved his car thirty feet from the tree just to be certain. The tree came crashing down exactly where he didn't want it, smack across the middle of his car, right between the front and rear door. And there it stayed.

I loved the cozy little place that was to be my home for a few months. It was one of the most perfect places I've ever lived. Complete solitude and a beautiful cold spring about twenty feet from the cabin. I was surrounded by old-growth timber of big fir and incense cedars. The cabin itself had one room with four windows, a tiny table, two chairs, and an iron bedstead, but no mattress.

No place has ever seemed so special to me. Many nights after I'd finished eating, I'd sit outside looking down the green, grassy glade. There was a little creek, and right in the middle of the other old-growth trees were two giant ponderosa pine trees, about as big as they get. In fact, those two trees are still there. Each evening, the deer would come to the glade to browse and drink from the creek. Many a night I sat there under the moon just watching and listening. So many creatures come out at night that one never sees by daylight. I never felt alone out there. It was the realization of everything splendid I had ever imagined.

Two weeks passed before I saw a single human. Then Ritter, a Forest Service ranger, appeared with ten enormous eastern brook trout packed in snow. He'd just caught them that morning. He and the dinner were most welcome. There was a purpose for his visit other than social, though. He'd come to take me to the Forest Service lookout on Table Mountain, a mile to the west. The regular lookout wouldn't be there for another couple of weeks and a fire could come along anytime. He taught me to use the alidade to pinpoint the smoke, and how to ring up the phone to give the daily report.

He also regaled me with stories, one of which turned out to be quite exciting for me. It seems that two years before, a man with several previous convictions had been arrested riding a stolen motorcycle on the Siskiyou Summit on Highway 99. He had confessed to stealing bikes in California and riding them up to a cabin near Hyatt Lake. There he repainted them, altered the serial numbers, and resold sold them in Oregon. No one had found that cabin. That was too much for my curiosity. Whenever I'd get back to my cabin with an hour or so of daylight left, I searched for his cabin. It didn't take me long to find it tucked away in a fir thicket, well hidden from view. It was only about six by eight feet, with a shed roof on one end. There were still two motorcycles in the shed and another one with no wheels propped up inside. The cabin itself was a work of art. The entire cabin, including roof and floors, was built from fir poles neatly notched and set in place with very few nails. It was completely covered with 'box shock,' the ponderosa or yellow pine boards that the mills produced for making shipping boxes for fruits and vegetables. Sometimes it came from the mill in rolls. It was thin, but strong. It had aged by this time and was the same gray color dead trees get once the bark is gone. Inside were a single-size, handmade bed, a small wood stove, and a table. In one corner there was a neat stack of over a hundred issues of the Saturday Evening Post, one of my favorite magazines. In those days, it was worth reading. I took six of them, and just in case he got out of jail, I left a note promising to return them. I had to respect the man in a way—the quality of his workmanship, the fact that he must have enjoyed solitude, too, and of course his choice of reading material.

One morning, I heard a car going up to Table Mountain. I knew it had to be the lookouts, George and Pearl Bossum. I loved my time alone, but I must admit, I was glad to have someone to talk with again.

There were some real characters on the lookouts, and they had to be in constant communication with one another. A Swedish immigrant name Petersen was one of them. He'd homesteaded near Big Draw Creek and Old Baldy. There was no lookout there and he wanted the job. The problem was the Forest Service had no money to build a lookout there. Petersen simply built his own. He chose one of the largest Shasta firs on the top of the mountain, and starting at the bottom, with a brace and a bit, bored holes in a spiral around the tree, each one a foot or so higher than the one before. He put Douglas fir pegs in the holes. I never went up to his platform, and I know of only two other men who dared climb up to it, but Petersen went up every single day and manned the phone around the clock.

I also got to know Hoyt Smith and his wife, the caretakers and operators of the Fish Lake Dam. Hoyt had two dangerous job. One was to take food and supplies to Ralph Cone, who lived year-round on top of Mt. Pitt (Mt. McLoughlin). To do this, he had to ride up an awesome trail that spiraled around the mountain a couple of times. His other responsibility was to let the water out of the dam as needed. Sadly enough, one evening when he and his wife went to let the water out of the dam, Hoyt walked out on the narrow board that led to the gate stock. The gate stock was a vertical shaft coming up from the gate below that alters the flow of water through the large pipe that goes out at the bottom of the dam. The walkway was only about eighteen inches wide, but it did have railings. Hoyt reached the end and called to his wife, whose back was to him at the time. When she turned, she saw that he was already being carried along into the boil of escaping water. He quickly disappeared. She drove to the Big Elk Ranger Station, and Ritter and the crew drove back as fast as they could. There was no sign of Hoyt at the outlet. Just after daylight the next morning, they found him about a mile and half below. Almost every bone in his body had been broken. No one knew what caused him to fall.

That summer I saw an ad in the *Ashland Tidings* for something I had plenty of—chipmunks. The address belonged to the clothing store in Ashland. They wanted a pair of live chipmunks and were willing to pay fifty cents for them. My Levi's were getting thin, and I could sure use that money. The chipmunks at the cabin weren't tame, but they'd come close enough to jump on my back, run across it, and jump off, so I had no trouble in catching two females and a male. I took them to the store, half expecting the owner to tell me it was a joke. Quite the contrary! He was delighted. He even took me to his home to show off the cages he'd made, complete with wheels to spin. But the highlight of my experience was the two pair of Levi's the man gave me, and the joy of listening to his brother-in-law play classical music on their piano. Music was not easy to find in my world of horses and cattle.

Later that summer Ritter rode up to tell me he was having a horse named Baboon brought up by one of the CCC (Civilian Conservation Corps) boys. The CCC was a government project designed to help thousands of young men around the nation who couldn't find jobs. Most of these men were from the city. Like new army-enlisted men, they were given U.S. Army equipment, tents, clothes, shoes, etc., and they lived in tent cities. The one near me was east of the Big Elk Ranger Station. Though supervised by Army lieutenants, the camps weren't military operations. The men worked at things like making trails, building wooden bridges, and fighting fires. They were paid a small salary, but they were allowed to search for outside jobs. If they found one, they could still eat and sleep in the camp. When the depression lifted, thousands of these young men found jobs, married, and stayed in the area.

Well, this particular CCC lad led Ritter to believe he knew horses. It was soon apparent he had exaggerated grossly. On the way up he'd gotten off the horse to relieve himself. Baboon was on the other end of a lead rope and had Ritter's saddle on his back. This young man let go of the lead rope, and Baboon, being no fool, recognized freedom when he saw it. He took off up the side of the mountain. He was right in the center of the land where he'd been born and raised. Obviously, this man didn't know the value of a horse. He rode up to the pasture ranch, showing no concern at all for the loss. After all, it was just a horse, wasn't it?

I looked for Baboon until dark, then gave up. I wasn't eager to invite the man for dinner. I loved eating alone, and I wasn't keen on keeping company with him after what he'd done, but I took him back to the cabin and cooked what I thought was a good meal. He loaded his plate with over half of the pot, gobbled it up, and then complained that there wasn't more for him. In the morning I fed him again and sent him on back to Big Elk. I rode up to the Table Mountain Lookout and had them put in a call to tell Ritter what had happened. Then I went searching for Baboon again. I was especially worried because he had a saddle on. A loose horse with a saddle could be in serious trouble if the saddle were to work loose and slip under the horse's belly. He'll actually run himself to death trying to kick it off. I knew that Baboon used to graze at Fred Henry's homestead, so that was the first place I went. Henry offered to help. It wasn't going to be an easy job. The country was full of timber, steep gullies, and thick brush patches. We could ride within a hundred feet of a horse and never see it. I wasn't much of a tracker either. The day passed with no trace of Baboon, so I went home to get some sleep. Just as I was getting ready to ride out again in the morning, here came Fred leading Baboon. Fred had found him by following the trail made by the dragging lead rope. He showed me where Baboon had tried to rid himself of the saddle by rolling on it, but he'd only succeeded in skinning up Ritter's saddle.

Baboon was unusually sociable. Whenever I rode him out, he was always eager to get back to the other horses. Too eager! One afternoon I rode him up the steep, mile-and-a-half long trail to

George and Pearl's on the lookout. It was too steep to ride straight up, so I had to zigzag up and around the timber and rock ledges. About twenty feet from the top, I tied Baboon to a tree and went on up to have dinner with my friends. By the time I left their place it was dark, but a full moon brightened the sky. Baboon was stomping and whinnying, obviously impatient to go home. From where we were, the trail went down over a small ledge and then bent off to the right into a leg of the zigzag. We'd gone about a hundred feet, when I suddenly had the strangest feeling come over me. It was a combination of absolute terror and at the same time a feeling of euphoria and exhilaration. Seconds later, Baboon, instead of turning to the right, jumped over the ledge and took off at a dead run straight down the mountain. He only had a snaffle bit on him, and I knew if I pulled the reins I'd cause him to roll over. I just sat back and prepared to enjoy the ride. It was spectacular. Way down below I could see the lake shimmering in the moonlight. Groves of trees flashed by. A few times he shot right through the pitch black of a grove. The entire ride couldn't have taken more than three minutes. We slid down onto the road and stopped exactly at the gate. Baboon called to the other horses. I unsaddled him, and he ran out to them as if such a run was an everyday occurrence.

It's unexplainable to this day—that glorious experience. Baboon was exceptionally agile, the best horse I could have been on. Many times I've relived that incredible ride and the mysterious sensations I felt. The morning after, I was so curious that I rode another horse partway up the mountain, and then by foot went over to where we'd come down. It was impressive: we'd sailed over six- and eight-foot ledges. At one place, I measured over thirty feet between one leap and the next hoof mark. After sixty years this is still one of the highlights of my life's memories.

In September the ranchers began taking some of their cattle out, and since I knew where the cattle were, I went along to help. One morning as we were going out, one of the ranchers reminded us that we were in Ritter's territory and he allowed no smoking. One of the men ignored the warning and continued smoking his corncob pipe. When Ritter drove up in the Forest Service truck, the old man hurriedly put his pipe in his overcoat pocket. The rest of us were talking with Ritter, when suddenly the old man let out a yell, jumped off his horse, and stumbled down to the lake, leaving a trail of smoke behind. At first he tried to take off his coat, but in the end he flung himself in the water—clothes, shoes, and all. No one said a word. Not even Ritter. He just wished the cattlemen luck in finding their cattle and drove off.

Mornings were cool at our elevation. A rain squall could bring as much snow as 'the Pitt' would get at one time. I hate to hear Mt. Pitt called Mt. McLaughlin. Ever since the first settlers the mountain was known as Mt. Pitt, named for John Pitt, one of the earliest explorers in the Sierras. He was one of the first to climb Mt. Shasta. In his journal he mentioned that due north he could see another snow-covered peak that looked to be almost as tall as the mountain he was on. When the settlers came to southern Oregon, they knew immediately this was the mountain Pitt had seen. Hence the name and why all of us old-timers call it the Pitt. Not many years ago our Congress, having nothing better to do, renamed it Mt. McLaughlin after the Hudson's Bay Company superintendent at Vancouver, Washington, when the British were there. There is no question McLaughlin was helpful to the first covered wagon folks, but he never came closer to that mountain than the Columbia River. It may cause confusion, but I, for one, refuse to call it anything but the Pitt.

There was not one day that September that I wasn't riding and shoeing a horse. One of the horses I had to shoe was a ten-year-old roan that had accumulated a number of bad habits from former abuse. I got a nasty gash from trying to shoe him. Since I had no way to bandage it, I had blood-soaked pants for days.

I'm adamant about natural healing methods. People look at me with disbelief when I tell them how I treat cuts. When I was a kid I had numerous cuts and many trips to the doctor. He always used the same so-called remedy: tincture of iodine. It stung like crazy. It may have killed germs, but it also killed the good bacteria and ruined the flesh. A deep cut could take months to heal, and the edges simply wouldn't join together. As soon as I arrived in eastern Oregon, I was given this advice: Never bandage a cut. If it's very large or deep, get on your horse and get to a doctor if you can. Anything else is treated with your own saliva and air exposure. Your saliva is an antiseptic, and the air hastens healing. It makes sense. All the animals do it. If they can reach the wound with their tongues, they rarely develop an infection. However, a deep puncture is different.

The number one fear in my work was horse manure, since it can cause gangrene, and that's nothing to fool with. If an open wound was exposed to manure, we had to watch for swelling in the lymph nodes or a red streak running up the arm or leg. Frequently, if this developed, amputation was the only cure. I saw a sad example of this. A young teenager got a compound fracture when she fell off a horse. Her doctor did an excellent job of setting the fracture. He then applied something to the puncture and put a cast on the arm. By the next morning her arm was very painful, and grew more so as the day went on. She developed a fever, and that night the doctor amputated the arm at the shoulder joint. She lived, but what a shame.

I know another story too A friend of mine called a young veterinarian to treat his seven-month-pregnant, purebred Arabian mare who had a barbed wire cut on the fetlock joint on her front leg. There is little else but skin there, and the cut was about a third of the circumference. The vet put some liquid on it and then a tight bandage with many layers. My friend asked me to have a look at it. The first thing I asked was if she had licked it clean. He assured me she had, but he figured he should have a vet look at her, since she was so valuable. I told him I'd seen a lot of wire cuts, but we'd never covered anything a horse could reach to lick. The following day the leg was completely swollen and the horse was suffering. The vet changed the bandages again. The next day she gave birth to a pre-mature dead colt. The mare was dead as well.

It was October before I could finally come down off the mountain. It had been a summer of isolation, with plenty of time to think about my future. I was ready to change my career, but what was I to do? I felt certain that I'd gotten a better education through my experiences than had I gone to college, yet I had no marketable skills other than my knowledge of horses and ranch life. I also knew I had something more important than anything else I could think of: the ability to be happy in solitude. By nature I'm not a solitary person, not a complete loner. But I knew that I could never live in a city. I would never feel at home there. Whatever I decided to do,

I needed to be independent and I needed to live in nature. I would have to have a skill to make this possible, a tangible skill—like silver working. There were surely enough horsemen who still admired the Spanish-style, highly decorated silver gear, and silversmithing seemed to come naturally to me.

I had no idea when I chose that career that some of my ancestors were well known for their silver work. I now have a biography of one of them who made and engraved the large silver buckles and double row of silver buttons on George Washington's inaugural clothes—his waistcoat and shoes.

I've often thought that perhaps this ancestor stands behind me, guiding my hand. I've never had a book or any help with laying out designs, but found it came quite easy with practice, and admittedly, much erasing.

I came to the carefully considered conclusion that I would now change from horses to a trade I needed to learn a lot more about before I could do it well enough to make a living.

Chapter 8

Rodeo Riding

Though I'd decided to work with silver, I still needed to earn money, and riding in rodeos would be a way of earning a few dollars. I'd grown disgusted with the way I'd seen horses being treated. A lot of people think rodeo riding is cruel to the horses, but I always tell them that it's a lot crueler to the men riding them than it is to the horses.

I rode in three rodeos in 1932. The first was the annual rodeo in Red Bluff, California. At the time, riding the bulls and bareback riding were not separate events. There were two pens, one full of horses and one full of bulls. Each pen had its own chute. Whenever there was a break in the main event, someone could run and get on a bull or a horse. Either one would come out bucking. The object was to stay on until the creature crossed the white chalk line a hundred feet into the arena. If the rider lasted, he earned a dollar, which in those days was an average day's wage. The saying was, "A dollar a day, a million days, a million dollars."

On one occasion, the bull I was riding stumbled just before the line and was down on his side for a second. I fell off and the bull got up and jabbed me hard. The sharp end of his horn went in between my leg bone and the muscles of my right leg. The pain was so intense, I could barely walk. At that time riders were required to sign a release in order to get an identification number and be able to ride, and there were no provisions for anyone wounded to get help. So despite my excruciating pain, I had to hang around until the end of the rodeo to get paid. I need not have wasted my time. The promoter had skipped out with all the gate receipts. That was not the first time that happened. Many riders lost this way throughout the years. To make matters worse, I'd hitched a ride to the rodeo with a man who had a horse racing at the track. We'd arranged to meet at a restaurant at seven that evening. I didn't get the dollar owed me from the rodeo, and I only had fifteen cents in my pocket, which wasn't going to get me far. At seven I dragged myself out to meet my ride, but he wasn't there. I got a cup of coffee and hobbled outside to wait. By ten o'clock most of the customers had gone, so I struggled back inside for another cup of coffee. I couldn't take the chance of waiting inside, in case I missed my ride. I knew that if he didn't see me, he'd just keep on going. By now my leg was so swollen it was getting tight in my pant leg, and the pain was getting worse every minute. At midnight I went back in and laid down my last nickel. A curious waitress asked me what had happened. My sad story moved her enough to offer me a free meal, and despite my pride and embarrassment, I was hungry enough to accept. My ride finally showed up at daybreak, hung over and barely able to drive. It was a long, scary, miserable trip home, and my leg took a long, miserable time to heal.

Lester Hicks told me of another rodeo that sounded promising. It was to be a three-day affair, and he assured me I'd earn good money. It was the brainstorm of the Klamath merchants and City Council, a way of bringing in some money to the town. The Klamath Falls Taxi Company agreed to sponsor it. Hicks was in charge of the livestock and the events. Many local ranchers provided bulls and bareback and saddle horses.

I grabbed my saddle and gear and arrived the day before the rodeo. Lester was riding the same sorrel that had climbed up my back and knocked me out years before when I was riding for George Noble. Lester told me what had happened to the sorrel since that day. Noble had sold him to Charlie, a local rancher. He and some of his help were riding out for their cattle, when they decided to stop at a cabin to buy some coffee from the Irish sheep rancher they knew. About fifty feet from the cabin, the sorrel suddenly shied and jumped. He tangled a foot and fell over on his side. Both man and horse got up. Charlie led the sorrel to the cabin, tied him to a tree, and sat down with his back against the deck. The Irishman obliged, got them a big pot of coffee, and told them to come and get it. They did. All but Charlie. One of the men shook him, and he fell over—dead. They called the local sheriff, who hurried out with a doctor to act as coroner. The doctor examined the corpse, and without a word, jumped back into his car and drove out of there. In short order he returned, bringing with him another doctor and the deputy. He'd found a deep fracture of the skull "done by a smooth object like a club," he said. Both doctors agreed Charlie's death was instantaneous. They also agreed that it couldn't have happened in the fall, else how could he have gotten up, let alone led his horse and tied him to a tree. "Someone must have hit him after he sat down," they said. The case was never proven and the cause was eventually established as Death Undetermined. "And now I'm riding a dead man's sorrel and wearing a dead man's boots," Lester told me. Charlie's widow had given Lester both the horse and Charlie's brand new boots.

It looked to me like it would be a successful rodeo. It included a roping exhibition performed in the middle of the four-hour program each of the three days by Alex Tecumpseh, a locally famous Klamath Indian roper. That had to be a big hit. Alex was born with both legs only about a foot long. He walked with difficulty, but once he was in the saddle, he was right at home. He had no stirrups, but his balance was perfect. I was to be part of his act. For my role, I was given a very well kept, gentle bay gelding to ride. My part was simple enough. All I had to do was gallop the bay past Alex in a straight line.

"The bay is trained to stop the minute I catch you. The horse knows what to do. You just stay on him and don't try to jerk him around," Alex told me. "I'll ride out into the middle of the arena, swinging my loop. You ride past me eight or ten feet away and watch what happens." Sure enough, the minute I felt the loop catch, the bay slid to a stop. At that point I was to turn to face the grandstand so the audience could see the white rope in a figure eight around my shoulders and around both the bay's front legs. Alex would take the rope off and the bay would run again. This time, Alex looped a figure eight around my neck and my foot in the stirrup. The loop had gone under the bay's belly and caught my foot on the other side. Then I held both arms out, and Alex looped the figure eight around both arms crossed on my chest. In another trick he looped all four of the bay's feet, one at a time. He'd trained the horse to sit down on his hind legs and slide to a stop. In three days, Alex missed only one throw.

I was especially excited about the fact that in this rodeo the bull riders not only were to get the mount money, but we'd be judged. The three best riders would get a first, second, and third place cash prize. We were given three bulls to ride each day. Only one other man and I rode all three, and the last day we were tied for first place. After we'd both ridden two bulls, we were still tied. By this time, we'd become friends and were cheering each other on. Neither of us was allowed to choose the third bull. We had to take whatever bull was in the chute. As soon as my competition's bull came out, it was obvious the bull was no good. He bucked, but not hard enough. My bull was just the opposite. I managed to ride him out, but it took all I had. There were no six-second rides then. We stayed on until the bull decided to stop. My bull took ten seconds before he quit. I was the winner, but had the bulls been switched, I knew my rival would have won. I'd noticed that he always went to a car in back of the arena, so this time I followed him. There he was changing into an Oregon State policeman's uniform. He told me he'd been raised in Pendleton and that riding bulls was his hobby.

After the rodeo, we all went to the taxi service window to collect our earnings. The office was vacated. Everything was gone. Not a scrap of paper. Nothing! Two old taxis sat out front, neither one in running condition. We'd been taken once again. There was nothing to do but go back to where I was staying and go to bed.

The next morning I met Lester at the rodeo grounds. "Skeet, I want you to know I didn't know anything about the SOB's taking off with the money. Everyone thinks I did, but I didn't. I was promised a good cut myself, but I didn't get a penny. Not one cent! Are you going to be okay?" he asked me.

I told him my only problem was that I had my saddle with me, but no way of getting home. Lester got off the sorrel, yanked the saddle off and gave me the reins. "Take the sorrel," he told me. "Sell him and keep whatever he brings." It took me two days to ride back to Ashland. By then I'd forgiven the sorrel for using my back for a ladder. Billy Timms, a young black man from Klamath Falls, had attempted to ride the bulls at that rodeo. He wasn't much good and he'd come to me for instructions. He was a tall, well-built, friendly man and I liked him immediately. We were both interested in a rodeo we heard was to be held at the fairgrounds in Grants Pass. It was going to be a small, but good, two-day rodeo. Billy and another rider, Billy Stepp, walked most of the way from Klamath Falls to Ashland to meet me. They'd spent one night up on the Green Springs in a wigwam burner—a twenty-foot-tall, conical-shaped, metal structure for burning the sawdust and refuse from the sawmills.

They were mighty grateful for a ride to Grants Pass in my father's Studabaker. When we got to the fairgrounds, we were informed that as participants we could sleep in one of the stalls reserved for racehorses. We didn't mind, since there was plenty of clean straw for bedding. There were fire rings to cook on, and I'd brought along cookware. Among us, we only had a little over a dollar. I suggested we buy a large box of pancake mix and some Crisco for frying. We could pick blackberries for nothing. Just then a young Klamath Indian showed up and asked if he could join us. He added fifty cents to the collection. I stayed to keep an eye on our things while the others went off in search of pancake mix and Crisco. We were already eating the pancakes when the Indian returned, struggling to carry bags of food. Obviously, he'd faced the situation before and knew quite well how to cope. He'd visited the local bakeries and asked for their stale bread and pastries. They'd given him enough for a week. This young man had been on the road five days, and except for twenty-five miles, he'd walked all the way from Chiloquin.

The next day we added rejected fruits and vegetables from a local cannery to our pantry. Fortunately, we all got along and we were all fairly successful at the rodeo. My three friends had been bucked off a number of times, but the money they were due was worth their bodies aching. Only none of us got the money. Same old story! It was devastating—not one penny for two days of risky, hard work. We moped back, sat around the fire, and ate in silence. On top of it all, my good, green, Hudson's Bay wool blanket had been stolen out of my bedroll.

We skipped the singing and storytelling, and quietly went to sleep that night. At one in the morning, Billy Timms woke me and whispered that I should follow him. I had no idea what was going on, but I pulled on my boots and followed him to the top tier of the grandstand. There an almost full moon shone brightly down on us and a huge watermelon was waiting to be eaten. I burst out laughing. I didn't ask where it had come from, and Billy didn't offer to tell me. We just sat back and enjoyed the sweet, delicious melon and the peaceful, warm summer night. The moon was so bright we could see every seed in the melon. We talked until there wasn't much left of the moonlight or the melon and for a while we forgot about being cheated. I learned how quickly one can bounce back and how little it takes.

A week after that rodeo, Billy Timms, Jess Stahl (the famous black exhibition rider), and two other riders stopped in Ashland to see if I wanted to join them. They were on their way to learn about a program to stop the cheating that occurred at rodeos, leaving the riders without their pay. The program was the Cowboy's Turtle Association, an association of rodeo performers. As members, we would be told in advance which rodeos had bonded money. The merchants of each city were responsible for protecting the gate receipts. If the city didn't do this, that rodeo was boycotted. Members wore small turtle pins for identification, but by the time the program was in place and I got a card asking me to join, I was out of the rodeo business.

Chapter 9

Silver Working

That spring, between the money I'd saved and trading in my Buick Master Coupe, I managed to buy a good, secondhand, small Dodge truck. I drove it to Alturas, where John Rachford, a sixty-year-old saddle and harness maker, had a shop, and he was willing to let me set up my work bench there. I brought along a desk a neighbor had made for me. Rachford and I were good partners. He made the bridles and I added the silver. I also fashioned single and three-piece buckles to the hand-carved belts he made. Our busiest time of the year was in the spring, when ranchers brought in their harnesses to prepare for haying season.

It didn't take long for me to build a big enough business to support myself and rent a place of my own. My first real start came from two brothers who happened to be visiting from the Rogue Valley. They bought two of my silver-mounted bridles, but more important, they introduced me to a young blacksmith in Lake Creek. He made some excellent patterns that I knew would sell. He agreed to let me add the silver and engraving to his work. I had myself another partner.

One of my memories of that summer was the anniversary of the first settlers who came to Surprise Valley in Modoc County, California, where it joins Nevada on the east. There was a county fair that started off with a parade to be led by the oldest living settler, a little old lady in her eighties. She was prepared to ride a large brown horse. I watched as she was helped out of the car and led to her horse with a sidesaddle on it. "Crow bait," she said, when she saw the horse. "I'm not going to ride that old crow bait. Get me a good horse." Quite an argument followed. The old lady looked all the other horses over, and pointing to a beautiful tall buckskin horse that looked like it just couldn't wait to take off, and said, "I'll ride that one." The men tried to tell her it was too wild and she wouldn't be able to ride it. "The hell I can't," she yelled. She got her way. They saddled the horse and helped her on. There she was in her lovely black riding habit with the divided skirt, and could she ever ride! That horse was full of fire. He pranced and danced and reared up all the way down the street, working up quite a lather. I can still see that little hundred- and- ten-pound lady sitting up on that twelve-hundred-pound horse, waving and calling out to everyone on both sides. I'd never seen a more remarkable show of superb horsemanship.

There was a rodeo in Susanville, California that summer, and I was determined to go, not to ride this time, but to see if I could sell some of my bridles and belts there. I took my dog Pal with me. I'd be sleeping in my truck, and since I'd have over two hundred dollars worth of work with me, I figured Pal would be a good night watchman. I got there before the start of the rodeo and walked casually around with the bridles and belts slung over my shoulder. I knew my prices were good, but I didn't know they were that good. By evening I'd sold half of all I'd brought. The gates opened at ten the next morning, and by the time the rodeo began, I'd sold out. My pockets were filled with silver dollars. I certainly couldn't walk around the rodeo with all that money on me, so I stuck them under the floor mat in my truck and went back to watch the rodeo.

I knew better than to start back to Alturas at night; I'd be a sitting duck if anyone wanted to hold me up. Except for a few drunks stumbling around, the rodeo grounds were empty. I was afraid I might have been watched, so I took my bedroll and spread it out under my truck, hoping Pal would let me know if anyone came near. I also took my silver dollars with me. Sometime after midnight, I felt someone tugging my arm. There was enough starlight that I could see a drunken Indian lying beside me. "What do you want?" I asked him. "Some drinky drink," he said. "It's all gone," I said. He slowly crawled away. My marvelous watchdog never so much as whimpered, let alone offered a protective bark.

That rodeo sale boosted my faith in my ability to succeed in silver working. Besides being extremely critical of my own work, constantly analyzing and looking for ways to improve my skill in whatever the task might be, it also helped that times were improving: Sterling silver was almost thirty-five cents a troy ounce, and an ounce hammered and shaped would make a concho that I could sell for up to two dollars. With gasoline at ten cents a gallon, bread at ten cents a loaf, and sardines ten cents a can, two dollars was worth a good bit in 1934.

During my time in Alturas I joined the National Rifle Association. Their chapter had their own shooting gallery in the basement of a building on the main street. The owner was a gun enthusiast, and he'd had the gallery built with a hundred-yard range for .22-calibre rifles and pistols. At that time I had my fairly new and inexpensive .22 rifle, but it didn't have the accuracy of the Winchesters. They were considered the current best. I also had two pistols, a Stevens single-shot and a .22 Colt revolver. Then .22-caliber ammunition cost about twelve cents for a box of fifty. Because I didn't have a good rifle, I couldn't enter the matches, but I was able to enter, and even win, a three-county pistol match. There were NRA observers in Modoc, Lassen, and Shasta counties. All three shot at the same type of target and at the same distance, and all were timed by split-second watches. The times were for six shots at each target, with fifteen minutes between targets to relax, clean, and reload. The first 'slow fire' gave each about thirty seconds for the six shots. 'Time fire' was ten seconds for six more, and the 'fast rapid fire' was five seconds.

I was the only one shooting a revolver. It had to be manually cocked, while everyone else shot the popular .22-caliber Colt Woodsman or Marksman semi-automatic pistol. My wife still has that pistol, and her aim is nothing to laugh about either.

That spring I decided to visit my parents, who had moved to Phoenix, Arizona. I camped out the first night on Walker Lake, and in the morning I drove down to Tonapah. Though Nevada was large, its population was small. There were thousands of miles of dusty dirt and crushed rock roads, and too few people to pay the taxes for improvement. By the time I reached Gold Field, the scenery had changed considerably. Here, there were Joshua trees and cacti, though still few human habitations. I found the perfect place to camp for the night down a little road called Corn Creek. It even had an artesian well—a five-foot pipe with cold water pushing up a foot or so high. I was grateful for that well, since the few gas stations I'd found along the way charged almost as much for water as they did for gasoline.

The next morning I drove through Las Vegas. Back then it had just one main street which ran north and south. All the buildings had shed-like roofs over the sidewalks, and long wooden benches under the roofs. There were about a hundred people lying back on the benches. I swear I didn't see a single person walking, or even standing up. I went on out of town, over a hill and down, and there was the Colorado River. I was seeing things I'd never imagined I'd see. There was a ferry called the Ari-Vada (Arizona and Nevada), a floating platform that could take four cars at a time. On each side of the ferry was a Ford Model T engine that powered a six-foot paddlewheel operated by a father and son. It went all of three miles an hour.

Just beyond Kingman, Arizona I came up behind a bunch of cattle. I stopped to ask the buckaroos if there was a shorter way than going to Ashfork and down to Prescott. They sent me by way of Wickenburg. It wasn't a main road, but one the local ranchers used. It certainly saved a lot of dusty miles. I camped by a spring that night. After a supper of canned soup, I settled down for a peaceful night's sleep. It was anything but peaceful. In fact, it was one of the noisiest nights I've ever endured. Millions of insects chirping among the cottonwoods and shrubs, birds screeching and calling, and lizards, spiders, and large scorpions scurrying through dead leaves made an unbelievable racket. Then came the snake. That did it! I climbed out of my bedroll and moved into the car for the night. By morning all was quiet again. The drive through the desert made up for the noisy night. For miles and miles I saw all sorts of exquisite cacti in bloom.

A couple of days after arriving Phoenix, I took a few of my silver-mounted bridle bits to show to the buyers at Porter's Saddle Company. They were so impressed that they ordered several different models for their catalog and for their retail store in Phoenix. What a welcome order that was. My old Dodge was on its last legs and I needed money to replace it. As it turned out, though, my father offered to pay the difference on a trade-in on a new Sedan Delivery (a panel truck). Now I could haul all of my gear in style.

The first thing I did after returning to Alturas was to go see Raphael Gardener, the man in Lake Creek, Oregon who was making the bits for me. I got to know Raphael and his family very well. His father had come from Italy fifty years before and bought his land from the railroad. He was a skilled mason by trade, and the house he built proved his ability. The stonework throughout was beautiful. From one large rock he'd chiseled out a kitchen sink. Years later, at the age of forty-five, he sent to Italy for a wife. Maria was eighteen when she married Raphael's father. They had six children. His surname was Gardinieri, but I think it was the children who Anglicized it to Gardener. Raphael and his sister Lucy had bought a hundred acres adjoining their parents' farm, and since they were still paying for it, I knew Raphael would appreciate the money he could earn by helping me with the bits for Porter's Saddle Company. Raddy, as Raphael was called, and I worked well together. He built a small shop and a cabin for me to stay in while I was there. Since we had no electricity, we used an old gasoline engine to run our grinding and sanding wheel.

But it wasn't all work. Raddy and I also did a lot of deer hunting together. The limit was one mule deer or two blacktails. With the nearest meat market twenty-five miles away by dirt roads, hunting was essential. Two blacktails canned in quart jars would last almost a year. Raddy's meadow was full of deer. Unfortunately, the does would hide their fawns in the tall grass, and too often the horse-drawn mowers would come through and surprise them. By the time they jumped up, the sickle bar would have already taken a leg. When a doe was killed, Raddy's mother would adopt the fawn and raise it on cow's milk. At one time she had five fawns that followed her around like pets.

There were also some exciting experiences, some with unhappy endings. Rosalia, Raddy's sister, and her husband, Eric, a Swedish immigrant, had a homestead a few miles up Lake Creek. Eric's brother also had a homestead, a mile or so west of Lake Creek. I remember the day I was coming back from Medford when I saw a gathering of people at the Lake Creek Store. There had been an explosion that broke windows in several of the houses nearby, and everyone thought it had come from Rosalia and Eric's place. A road contractor had been blasting on what is now Highway 140. Before he shut down for the winter, he'd stored two hundred cases of dynamite and an iron chest full of dynamite caps and rolls of fuse in a building about a quarter of a mile from Eric's. He'd put a heavy padlock on the chest and posted DANGER, EXPLOSIVES on all four sides of the building.

We all flew up to the storage building, but all that was left was a crater about a hundred feet across, and dozens of bent and broken picks and shovels strewn about. The two inches of snow on the ground made it easy to see the human footprints coming up from Lake Creek, then going back down and finally disappearing in the crater. There were also footprints that reappeared on the other side, went up toward Eric's, then came back down again and entered the crater. We knew there had to be a body somewhere. The deputy asked for help.

First we found some pink and blue things on the snow about the size of a match head. It was human flesh and a piece of clothing. Then we found a piece of thick skin from a heel, a bit of scalp showing a haircut, part of a rib, and part of a breast bone. The coroner laid them out on a log, identified each piece, and with us as witness, announced that this evidence proved, "An unknown human had met death through a dynamite explosion on this day, week, month and year." He took a stick, scraped the pieces off the log, kicked some dirt over them and went home.

There was one bit of comic relief in that tragedy. Eric and his brother each thought the explosion had been at his brother's place, so they had both been in quite a turmoil until they found out otherwise. We never did find out who the victim of the explosion was.

In the meantime Raddy and I were in full production, turning out two silver-mounted bits a day. Things were going smoothly until the day I got the telegram saying my father was in critical condition. I ran out of the shop, jumped in my car, and drove to the airport, but since the banks were closed, the airlines wouldn't accept my check. I showed them the telegram and begged them to call several Medford businessmen who I knew would vouch for me, which they did. So there I was in the airplane in my dirty work clothes, surrounded by men in crisp business suits. I didn't even own a suit. I slunk as far down in my seat as my long legs would let me.

Sometime on that flight, the captain announced that Will Rogers had just died. My father had always been a fan of his, and I thought to myself: Perhaps now my father will have a chance to meet him.

My father died before I got there. Two days before his death, he'd had what was to be a simple hernia operation. He complained the night of his surgery of extreme pain, and then he just stopped breathing. He was only sixty-seven. This was a man who'd survived typhoid fever, pneumonia, and blood poisoning, all at a time when there were few remedies. This made his death from unexplainable cause more difficult to accept.

At the service a woman walked up to the coffin. Holding a large bouquet of flowers above her head, she said, "He was a royal gentleman." She laid the flowers down and walked away. I have no idea who she was, but she was right. He truly was a royal gentleman. And my mother was an equally royal gentlewoman.

I stayed with my mother for a week, and then went back to work. It was nearing the end of 1935 when Raddy and I took off for the brushy slopes of Esmond Mountain, where Raddy knew of a trail that would lead to a great hunting area. He didn't warn me about the eight-foot-high manzanita thickets we'd have to fight through. He was having trouble finding the trail, so when we saw a dead pine snag, Raddy hoisted me up until I could reach some dead limbs to see if I could spot it. I still had one foot on Raddy's shoulder, when he suddenly dropped right out from under me and started shooting. There I was hanging by one hand on the branch, with both of my legs kicking around in the air, and I hadn't the foggiest idea what was going on. I couldn't see a thing. What Raddy had seen was the largest bear either of us had ever seen—not ten feet from us.

Generally we wouldn't shoot a bear. Older ones aren't good eating, but this was a monster. He was so big that we had to get a couple of neighbors to help us drag him on a sled down to a road and onto my truck. We took him to Medford and had him weighed on registered scales. His weight of two hundred and eighty-seven pounds attracted a great deal of attention. A newspaper reporter took photographs, and then went through their files to see what might compare. In 1887 a brown bear weighing two hundred and ninety pounds had been killed, but he wasn't weighed on registered scales.

It was exciting, but we were still stuck with the question of what in the world we would do with the bear. The owner of a local market came to our rescue by offering Raddy twenty-five dollars for the bear and the rest to be taken out in trade from the market. Raddy accepted, and the bear was shipped to a dealer in San Francisco's Chinatown. When people asked me where I was when Raddy shot the bear, I answered truthfully, "Climbing a tree." It didn't give me much glory.

I've seen lots of bears since, but the only one I ever shot was a fat two-year-old. I had it made into smoked ham and bacon. The meat was good, but I much prefer seeing live bears. Brown bears aren't the least bit dangerous to humans. They come through here each fall and eat berries and camas bulbs. Apparently they eat the death camas, too, but this doesn't surprise me. I've heard that the first settlers claimed their pigs relished them. They're supposed to be poisonous to humans, but usually it just makes them very sick. (The species by our place here on the Rogue River are Zygadenus, with pale greenish-yellow flowers. The Camassia camas has blue to purple flowers, so they're easy to tell apart.)

One evening in March of 1936, Raddy and his brother Bennett ran to tell me that Lucy had gone into a diabetic coma and they needed me to take her to the hospital immediately. They had called the doctor, so she was expected. I had the only available car, and we knew I'd need help getting over the old wagon road that night because the pouring rain made the clay soil slippery as grease. It was so steep in places that we had to put on chains. Even so, our rear wheels slid into ditches several times. We'd have to lift the whole rear end up by the bumper and set it back on the road. Only one old nurse and an aide were there when we arrived at eleven that night. We carried Lucy to her room on a stretcher, and Raddy told the nurse to call the doctor right away. "I know how to handle this," she said. "I've done it many times. No reason to call the doctor at this late hour." She kept checking on Lucy and telling us she was doing just fine. Then at one o'clock, she realized her mistake. Ten minutes later, the doctor rushed in with his bag. As he went bounding up the stairs, he glared and pointed a finger at her. "God damn you! I told you that I was to be called the minute she got here." Twenty minutes later, Lucy was dead. "I could have saved her if I'd been called in time," the doctor told us. The old nurse was nowhere in sight.

Now that Lucy was gone, I knew Raddy would have to spend more time during the spring and summer months tending the ranch. He'd have little time to work with me. That meant I'd better look for a place of my own. A real estate agent directed me to some riverfront property on Old Ferry Road in what is now Shady Cove. At that time there was no town or post office there, only Crater Lake Highway, then just a gravel road. I was disappointed to find there was no road leading into the land, only a fence with no gate.

"But there's no problem," the realtor said. "Just buy it and the owner of the fenced land will have to give you a right-of-way. Or you could even go to the courthouse and they'll condemn a right-of-way through the other man's property."

That didn't seem a friendly way to begin, since we'd be neighbors, so I decided I'd go talk with the owner myself. Bristow was hostile at first, but when I told him I was looking for some land on the river to buy, he calmed right down. "We have a lot of land to sell," he said, pointing to a big one-word sign on the hill beyond his house: RIVERFRONTAGEFORSALE. "That sign's been there for four years and you're the first customer," he told me. Minutes later I was the owner of forty acres of river frontage, plus a two-story house, a good well, and a rock cellar for keeping vegetables and canned food from freezing in the winter. I agreed to let them stay for a couple of months while they built a new house on the lower end of their three forty-acre plots. In the meantime I'd stay at Lake Creek and continue working.

Chapter 10

Phoenix, Arizona

The following August I got another telegram. This one informed me that my mother was in Sacred Heart Hospital and she was doing fine, but she wanted very much to see me. Twenty minutes later I was on my way to Phoenix. Except for a couple of hours sleep in my car, I drove straight through. My mother was weak, but other than that I wasn't too concerned, especially after the doctor assured me that she'd be going home in two days and that a nurse would be staying with her until she was well again. It made sense for me to go back to Oregon for a week to settle things there and then return to stay with her myself.

It took me two days to get back to Lake Creek. I stopped at the Lake Creek Store to get my mail and there was a telegram that had arrived within the hour saying, "Your mother has just passed away. Doctor. . . August 20, 1937." I couldn't believe it. I read and reread that telegram, then climbed right back in my car, turned around, and headed back to Phoenix.

I stopped only to gas up. The last one hundred and fifty miles were torture. I tried every trick I knew to stay awake. I took a little tobacco from a cigarette and put a pinch in one eye. That burned so bad I couldn't possibly have fallen asleep at the wheel, but it wore off in twenty minutes. Then I'd put some in the other eye. Eventually that didn't work either, and besides, I was having trouble even seeing by then. Finally I stopped, got a large, heavy wrench, and held it in one hand against the steering wheel. That worked. If I dozed off and relaxed my grip, the wrench fell, making an awful clang and thump that woke me right up.

I finally drove into my parents' driveway at three in the morning. I had a key, but I couldn't get in because there was a large padlock on the door. I lit a match and read: Maricopa County – Sheriff's Office. Even the back door was padlocked. There was nothing to do but sleep in the car. I woke early in the afternoon with a stiff neck and a very empty stomach. I'd had nothing to eat or drink on the trip. It was then that I remembered my father saying that if anything should happen to them I should call their lawyer, a Mr. Allee.

With apologies, Mr. Allee explained the law I was faced with, and the reason the law was enacted. Arizona's year-round dry, warm climate brought thousands of people with tuberculosis hoping for a cure. Most came from the East Coast, and most of them bought a house. If and when they died, their heirs were required to live in the house for one calendar year before the heir could resell it. The heir himself had to live in it. As a result, the state was making piles of money, since most of the heirs had their business back east and they would simply forfeit their claim. This certainly didn't sound legal to me, but Mr. Allee told me in no uncertain terms that, if I decided to stay, I'd better not sneak out, because I'd be under constant surveillance. I said I'd stay, but first I needed the right to get in the house immediately. Mr. Allee got that permission for me.

Once in the house, I found a note my mother had left for me. A line from it said, "Your life can be beautiful. Live every golden moment of it." I also found a carefully wrapped package in her room with a note from the nursing sister who had been staying with her. It said that the rings, the watch, and the pendant in the package were the ones my mother was wearing when she died.

The phone rang constantly with offers of help from her friends, many of whom were members of the Daughters of the American Revolution. My mother was always proud that she was a two-star DAR. Her father, Edward Thomas Whittingham, was a physician and surgeon who during the Civil War was given an appointment on a parchment scroll signed by Abraham Lincoln and Secretary of War Edwin Stanton. After the war he returned to Millburn and resumed his practice. He died before I was born, but I was given his name.

I was so dazed by the sudden, unexpected death of my mother that I didn't realize until the day after my arrival that I was stuck in Phoenix and my tools were back in Oregon. Allee got permission for me to return for my tools since they were necessary for my subsistence. So then I had my tools, but no place to work. Since there was plenty of space behind the house, I decided to have a shop built there. After all, I had an entire year ahead of me. I answered a building contractor's ad and told him I wanted a twelve-by-twelve-foot wood building with lots of windows. Not only did he quote a price considerably less than I'd expected, but it included basic wiring and a promise to start the next morning. True to his word, he and his crew arrived early. I asked how long it would take. "I'll have it done by noon," he said. "This is my specialty. Whenever someone wants to put up a small building, you can be sure the neighbors will protest that it will spoil their view or some such excuse. I build it before the opposition has time to file a complaint." I'd found the right man. Even I knew that once a building is up, it could take years of litigation to have it removed. By mid afternoon I'd moved my forge, anvil, and silversmithing bench into my new shop. I was ready to go to work.

Before long I was spending twelve hours a day working on silver, and still I couldn't keep up with the orders. I had to find help. I hired someone who was recommended by a friend of my parents. Greg was a few years younger than me, strong, athletic, and seemingly tireless. Though he'd never worked with hacksaws and rasps, the tools I used to cut iron into the thickness and width needed for bits, he was eager to learn. He was also eager for the wages I paid him, which were much better than he'd earned as a common laborer. Greg's past was interesting and rather unusual. For generations his family had lived in Annapolis. His father was a retired admiral, his two older brothers were naval officers, and his sister was a nurse in the Navy. Of course, Greg wanted to graduate from the Naval Academy, having spent his growing years around ships and boats. He was not at all pleased when his father enrolled him in West Point, but nothing could change his father's mind. Because of the rivalry between the two services, Greg knew he was in for some hassling. Although he did well academically, he was miserable. The hazing never ceased at West Point, and when he came home, his brothers would start in. He had no respite, and the longer it continued, the less he wanted any part of it. He made up his mind to get himself expelled, and he did—two weeks before graduation. It was his duty to load and fire the cannon that started each new day. He decided to spice up the morning and rearrange his life by loading a brick on top of the wadding. The brick came out with a loud whistle and smashed smack into the wall several hundred feet away. Because it wasn't the first time someone had done that, Greg knew the consequences would be an immediate dismissal. With that brick he blew away four years and any future he might have had in the service, but he had no regrets. He packed his bags and moved to Phoenix to live with his sister and her husband until he found work.

Greg had learned to box at West Point, so I bought us each a pair of gloves, and he spent twenty minutes each day teaching me what he knew. Lucky for me we were boxing and not fighting—he was six feet tall and weighed a hundred and seventy pounds. I was only five-foot-ten and weighed a hundred and twenty.

I was interested in buying a motorcycle with a sidecar so I could tour the Northwest as soon as my year was up. In fact, I went so far as to go to a local shop to look them over. When they offered to give me a ride in one, I eagerly accepted. It was fun until I made the mistake of asking how it would do on dirt roads. He grinned, turned off onto an old plowed, but not yet harrowed, orange grove with deep furrows and ridges between them. Instead of slowing down, he opened it up and purposely turned and twisted around as we bumped over them, grazing some trees along the way. Needless to say, I was scared to death, and I didn't buy the thing.

Greg and I talked a lot about flying, and he began taking half-hour lessons at a small airfield north of Phoenix. The instructor charged five dollars an hour or two fifty for a half-hour lesson. Though I'd been in planes before, I never thought much about flying myself. I got hooked on planes accidently. I'd driven Greg out to the field for his lesson, and there was an old man selling rides in a plane—a cabin mono with side-by-side seating for two. The pilot, whose name I later learned was William Angel, strolled over and asked if I'd like a ride. I asked if he could fly over my place so I could see what it looked like from the air. Since it was only a couple of miles away, he agreed. On the way back, he asked me to take over so he could light his cigarette. No indeed, I told him, I've never flown before and I'm likely to have us upside down. He was so insistent, though, that I reluctantly agreed to try it. The plane had a set of controls in front of each of us. As I put my feet on the rudder pedals and my hand on the stick, he let go, reached for his cigarette, lighted it, and sat back. He was amazingly relaxed for someone in his position. I guess that gave me confidence, because I soon found myself enjoying the experience. He had me bank it one way, then the other, to show how easily it turned. Then he had me line it up with the runway while he throttled back, and we came gliding in. "Stay on," he said, "I promise I'll help you with the landing if you need me." I couldn't believe how easy and smooth it was. I thought about that ride the rest of the day and night.

A few days later I was back at the airfield. I couldn't find that pilot, but the young owner of the field offered to teach me to fly for fifty dollars. We agreed that I would take an hour lesson early in the morning before work for eight days—the minimum number of hours of dual instruction required by federal law before soloing. The next morning I had my first lesson in one of the new Taylor-Cubs with a 40–horsepower Continental engine. A few years later it was renamed the Piper Cub. It didn't take long to see that he was a good pilot, but he was one poor instructor. He boasted that he was the youngest commercial pilot west of the Mississippi, having attained that honor at just past sixteen years of age. His idea of teaching, though, was to do it and then say, "Just do what I did." Nevertheless, I persevered. Each morning I'd roll the plane out, unchock the wheels, and warm up the engine. Only then would the young man crawl out of bed, stumble outside, and climb in.

On the eighth morning, when he didn't show up at all, I went to his room and found him fast asleep. I woke him, but he wasn't about to get up. "Look," he mumbled, "I didn't get to bed until after four. You've had enough time in, take it up yourself." With that he rolled over and went back to sleep. I'd had exactly seven hours of training, but I'd be darned if I was going to let him hold me back. I climbed in, opened the throttle, and took off. The only thing that startled me was seeing the stick in front moving around alone. I was in the rear seat of the plane, so it looked like a ghost flying the plane up front. After taking off and making three good landings, I quit and went back to the instructor's room. He was still fast asleep, and that's how I left him.

When I returned to the shop and told Greg that I had just soloed my first airplane, he wouldn't believe me. To prove it, I went right back to the airfield, rented a plane for twenty minutes, and flew low over the shop so he could see for himself.

Apparently, Tom didn't find too much fault with his hasty lessons. According to Tom's youngest son Tim: Unbeknownst to Father, I bought a plane in 1978. The day the pilot flew my new Piper Cub in, I went to Father, told him I bought a plane, and asked if he'd teach me to fly. "Sure," he said, without a hesitation. We climbed in the plane, a taildragger, and started to taxi. Father hadn't been in a plane in some twenty years by then. He sat tandem in back of me, where it was hard to see. "Well," he said to me, "I'll show you what to expect. We'll do a fast taxi with the tail up. You pick out a tree and point at it." Then he gave it the gas, and there I was, staring at the tree. And there he was, flying in an absolutely straight line. It was incredible that he could fly like that when he'd been away from it for so long. It was like he never quit teaching. He taught me to fly and to solo, but of course I couldn't record any of it because it wasn't legal. It meant a lot to me to have my father teach me, though.

I learned more about silver smithing by accident. I was walking in an area of Phoenix where I'd never been before, when a tall young Mexican approached and asked where I'd gotten my belt with the engraved silver buckle on it. I told him I'd made it. After I'd taken it off and handed it to him, I wondered if I'd been crazy to trust this stranger. He could easily have run away with it, but he only looked it over carefully and asked how I'd done the engraving. He said he was a silversmith too, and he offered to show me where he worked. Again, I wondered whether I was too trusting and if I was being led into a trap, especially when he turned and led me down an alley to a back door. We entered a large room where four or five Hispanics sat at a bench, each with a plumber's gasoline blowtorch. Then I realized where I was. The building fronted on a major downtown street, where many items from Mexico and Central America were sold.

Ed Lugo, my new acquaintance, was the foreman of the shop. He spoke English well. In fact, most of the men were bilingual.

The owner, Arturo Lemon was a sixty-year-old Hispanic, a very courteous man. As it turned out, I spent a great deal of time with those men during my year in Phoenix, learning not only about silver smithing, but also about their culture. I was surprised to learn that none of the Southwest Indian tribes originally made silver jewelry, with or without turquoise or other stones. Instead, it was made by the Mexicans. History confirms that California, Arizona, New Mexico, and Texas were originally settled in those places by Mexicans, and the Mexicans, since the days of the Mayans and Aztecs, have been known as fine silver and goldsmiths. I often saw Mexicans pretending to be Navajo while they sat cross-legged on the sidewalks selling their jewelry.

Ed showed me how they silver-soldered the tiny joints on their jewelry with the gasoline torches. It was a valuable lesson for me. Other silversmiths used a small concentrated alcohol butane torch, but these men, with no knowledge of engraving or rough finishing and polishing, were using something that looked liked overkill, easily doing something that was difficult for me to do, even though I used a much more expensive and seemingly better torch.

Ed also told me that the bulk of the silver his men were using was made of Mexican pesos, about the size of our silver dollars. They were sold in a place called Miller's Assay Office in Nogales on the border. Sixteen feet of the Assay office was located in Arizona and ten feet in Mexico. I bought Ed and myself each a hundred pesos, and paid for them in the part of the building that stood in the United States. The pesos cost thirty-three and a half cents, or three for a dollar. After the man collected my money, he walked the few feet back into Mexico and put the pesos in a canvas bag for me. Each peso had what looked like a date embossed on it, usually 1943, 1944, or 1946, but those numbers were actually the content of pure silver. The rest was an alloy, mostly copper. Pure silver is much too soft to use as a coin or in jewelry. It can be scratched or bent almost as easily as lead. It's the alloy that makes it usable.

Ed took me to another silversmith shop in Phoenix to show me how they annealed the coins and ran them through a hand-cranked roller to whatever thickness they wanted. They would then scrape and sand the lines made by the printing and the figures on the coins. It was a lot less expensive than buying sterling for jewelry making, and it looked and wore just like sterling.

Silver jewelry designed and made by Tom.

Above. Details of a 1904 octagon barrel 22
Shorts Marlin Rifle. Silver work designed
by Tom. Right. Silver lighter designed and
made by Tom.

The art of direct salesmanship was another lesson Ed taught me. We both made a variety of a dozen or so rings and took them into a restaurant. We ordered pie and coffee, then dumped our rings all over the counter and appeared to be examining them. Of course, the waitress couldn't keep her eyes off of them. We were selling the rings for a dollar each. The same rings would have cost three to five dollars in a retail store. She bought one immediately, and by the time we left, we'd sold five more. We were equally successful in the next two restaurants, but in the meantime, we'd eaten three pieces of pie and we'd drunk three cups of coffee.

As much as I hated the fact that I was forced to live in Phoenix for a year, it was an instructive year. I had many interesting experiences. Pinky Gist provided me with some of them. Pinky was using his small, well-trained mules in a comedy act at the Arizona Biltmore Hotel, and he came to me about some work for the mules' gear. He invited me to the Biltmore to watch him in a staged rodeo and to see Doc Pardee, a top rodeo performer, who was riding and roping in the same rodeo. After that, I went often.

The Biltmore, a beautiful building surrounded by luxurious grounds north of Phoenix, had a flock of sheep in the middle of the orange and grapefruit groves. It included a sheepherder authentically garbed, including a sheep hook, for the patrons' enjoyment. I got to know Tom, the sheepherder, and he, too, had an unusual story. He told me how, at twenty, he'd been diagnosed with tuberculosis and how his parents had scraped together enough money so he could leave New York City and come to Arizona for his health. He loved Arizona, but because he couldn't make enough money to live on there, he decided to walk across the border into Mexico. He was a religious man, and he got into the habit of touching the heads of children and blessing them as he made his way through the countryside to the border. Since he had little to wear except a hospital robe and he hadn't had a haircut in ages, he presented a rather saintly picture. Often he'd be invited to have a meal and spend the night with strangers.

Sometimes it would be in a house, but just as often in a shack or a lean-to. In the mornings he'd bless the family and be on his way. By the time he got to Mexico, he felt almost cured. He lived there for two and a half years and then slowly retraced his steps back to Arizona. According to a local doctor, he was in complete remission. The doctor's theory was that he was cured because he was living, for the most part, outdoors and breathing good air unbreathed by countless other people.

I agree with that doctor. The last flu or cold I had was thirty-eight years ago when my children stopped bringing the bugs home from school. I'm certain it's also because I see so few people, and because up until 1992, except for three nights, I spent seventeen years sleeping outside through all kinds of weather and seasons. Elva and I put a sturdy metal bed just outside our kitchen facing the Rogue River. Except in the winter, when we used an opened sleeping bag made of down to cover us, we used regular bedding. I fashioned a canopy, using fir poles as uprights, and I extended a tarp over the canopy wide enough to keep the rain and snow from dripping on us. I must admit, we weren't sleeping out there in 1948 when it was seven degrees below and the river froze over. Nor were we out there a couple of years ago when it got to seventeen below and people in Gold Hill could walk across the Rogue River. It's been cold, but never that cold since then. Elva gave up sleeping outside a few years before I did.

Tom didn't say why Elva quit sleeping outside with him, but she was not shy about the reason: "I slept outside with Tom until he kicked me out. Not that he did it on purpose, but he'd roll over on my side of the bed, and when I complained, he'd tell me to go around and climb in on his side. I told him if I couldn't sleep on my own side of the bed, I wasn't going to sleep out there. And I didn't. Now I sleep in my bedroom with the windows open so the bats can come in. I love to watch them fly around. I don't know why people are afraid of them. They're good to have around. They eat all the flies and insects, and by morning they're gone again. I loved sleeping outside though. We started sleeping out there after the boys grew up and left the house. Tom slept out there in all kinds of weather all year round – lightning, snow, no matter what. Not me. I'd come in as soon as it started lightning. We had a buck hanging around here for several years. It got so I could hold a piece of bread in my hand, lie real still, and he'd come right up and eat it from my hand. I miss that part of it."

One thing about living and working in Phoenix that took some getting used to was the oppressive Phoenix heat. Outdoor workers began at daylight, worked four or five hours, quit until four o'clock, then worked again until dark. Some days my thermometer in the shade showed a hundred and twenty degrees. During the hottest months I put a carboy (a five-gallon glass jug made for holding acid) of water on a stand I made. Greg and I regularly drank it dry by noon. We'd refill and empty it again by five. These acid jugs, made for muriatic and sulphuric acids, were water soluble and only needed a good wash out before using. Greg and I both lost weight during those months. Old-timers warned us to drink only tepid water, never ice cold, and certainly never drink cold beer, wine, or sodas. Drinking cold sodas or beer in such heat could lead to severe kidney and bladder problems. To this day I still drink about a half gallon of water a day, and always at room temperature.

It was a lucky day for me the day I met Ernest Sink, better known as Red Sink because of his red hair. He was about my age, and he was an excellent flight instructor. Red told me about another airport where I could rent a plane for less money. It was owned by a rancher named Robert Fram. Flying was Fram's hobby and he was an excellent pilot and instructor. He gave me a check ride in a larger plane than I'd ever flown. After two landings, he had me solo. It was a most unusual landing field, and I was somewhat apprehensive. We took off toward the west, right over a solid row of trees. The moment the wheels left the ground, I had to make a ninety-degree turn to the right for a couple hundred yards, then a turn to the left at the end of the row of trees. Coming in to land, I had to follow the same pattern, but in reverse. It took me a couple of passes to get used to that.

It was Fram who taught me how to recover from a spin. First of all, the cost of a plane rental is set by the cost of the plane and the horsepower of the engine. The cheapest plane he had was a Porterfield Zepher with a forty horsepower engine. It flew well, but because of the small engine it had very little climbing ability with two people aboard. Nevertheless, we took off climbing to three thousand feet, a necessary altitude for spin and recovery practice. Only we never even got to a thousand feet. We had to go back and land. Fram then explained the procedure to me and told me to try it on my own. I was nervous as hell. A plane in a spin is diving down at a steep angle and spinning rapidly. Fram watched as I got in the Zepher and took off. I climbed to three thousand feet and then started repeating out loud what he'd said to do: *Pull the throttle back. Put the nose up in a climb. When the nose starts to fall, pull the stick back hard. Hold it there and push the left rudder pedal all the way and hold it. To recover, get off the rudder pedal. Put the stick ahead. When the spin stops, pull back until the ship is level.* It worked. The first time was terrifying. I climbed back up and did it again, this time even letting it spin a little longer. That was a lesson worth learning.

William Angel, the pilot who first handed me the controls while he lit the cigarette, came over to Fram's field and gave me some dual instructions. He signed my log book, which I still have. His brother was Eddie Angel, the man who discovered Angel Falls in South America.

What had begun as just a break in the daily grind was becoming a fascinating hobby, even an obsession. Airplanes occupied most of my thoughts. I took more dual instructions with Red Sink. I was thrilled the first time I soloed a Taylor Craft, a two-place, side-by-side monoplane.

I was even more thrilled the day Greg and I saw Tex Rankin in an air show in Phoenix. Rankin held the number one spot in the international aerobatics competition. Little did I know then how much time I'd be spending with him in the future. Sadly, we saw something that wasn't much fun to watch that day. There was a special event that featured a man wearing homemade bird-shaped wings that he was trying out for the first time. He sat inside a large cargo plane, perching himself on the edge of the wide, open doors of the fuselage on the left side, his legs dangling outside the plane. His wings were strapped on him and stretched out on each side just inside the plane, out of the wind. When they got to three thousand feet, they flew him past the spectators. When he was just opposite where we all were standing, he fell forward, and his wings stretched out fine, but only for a second. We could see some sort of fabric connected to each leg—a kind of tail that made him look even more like a bird as he dove down at a forty-five degree angle for a hundred feet. Suddenly, he went into a spiral that became a violent spin within seconds. Instead of coming straight down, he veered off to the west and right into the tops of a row of cottonwood trees. He bounced off the trees, into the power lines, and fell to the ground. He was rushed off in an ambulance. Before the end of the air show, they announced that he'd dislocated both shoulders, but he'd live.

As well as learning to fly, I continued to learn more and more about jewelry making. I was even offered a teaching job before I left Phoenix. Noel, the eighteen-year-old son of a blacksmith instructor at an Indian School on a U.S. Army Post, often hung around our shop. He'd had polio as a child and was left with a limp and only one good arm. Noel invited me to visit the school. Orphaned Indian youths from ages two to eighteen were housed in large dormitories on the post. They were taught trades so they could eventually earn a living. They'd come from different tribes and came knowing only their own native language, so they had to learn English before anything else.

I was curious about a full-size basketball court I'd seen as I drove in. The entire fence, including the swinging gates, was made of inverted U-shaped pieces of round iron welded together in alternate rows. The two bottom ends of one inverted U were welded to the center of two pieces below, small enough that a basketball couldn't go through. I was shocked when they told me it was made of brand new barrels from the Springfield Army .45-.70 caliber rifles. I shook my head and moaned. What a waste! I'd traded my .45-.70 when I got my new .30-.30 Winchester. Now I wish I had it back. It had been getting good reviews as a very accurate, well-made single shot. When I left the school, I noticed an old blanket folded in the back of my truck, but I didn't bother with it until I got home. There under the blanket, in its original factory box, was a brand new .45-.70 caliber Springfield rifle, the same kind of rifle carried by General Custer's troops when they were wiped out at the Battle of Little Bighorn in 1876.

I appreciated the offer to remain and teach at the school, but there was no way was I going to stay in Arizona. The cool, green mountains and the rivers and lakes of Oregon was where I belonged. As for Greg, we kept in touch through letters for several years. He joined the Marines, was in charge of anti-aircraft, and moved up the ladder quickly. The last I heard, he was back in Annapolis, Maryland and into sailboats.

Chapter 11

Medford Flying

In August I was free at last to go home. I still had to sell the house, and I wanted to do it before I left the state. I hired a moving company to take my parents' furniture to my place in Oregon, and I donated their large collection of books to a library. The realtor assured me he could sell the house in one or two days, but suggested I wait until winter, when I'd get more money for it. Never mind the money, I told him, sell it. True to his word, he had the house sold by four o'clock the first afternoon and I was on my way.

The day I arrived home, I went right down to the river and caught a couple of trout to add to my potato and the bacon I cooked on my old cast-iron cooking stove that also doubled for heat.

First thing the next morning, I asked Mr. Bristow, the man who sold me the house, to build a new workshop for me and to use rough lumber, since it would soon be coated with smoke from my forge anyway. I bought a good second-hand oxygen-acetylene welding outfit. Soon I was back at work making silver jewelry. I also sold native gem stones. I didn't make much, but at least I didn't have to split the profits with anyone.

I also didn't have anyone to talk with, and though I loved my solitude, I did get tired of talking to myself after awhile. I found a dog at the pound who filled that gap. It was love at first sight. This skinny, little, black and white dog came bounding over to me, wagging her tail and jumping up and down. Powder and I became immediate and fast friends. I almost lost her to salmon poisoning the following year. She crawled under the house and wouldn't let me near her. No matter how I begged, she wouldn't budge. On the seventh day, I heard a feeble little whine and she came dragging herself out. It took another week before she was fully recovered. Salmon poisoning is a common cause of dog deaths along the river. Thousands of salmon come up the river to spawn, then die, leaving their carcasses to line the banks in the fall. A local vet told me a dog has only to lick one of the dead salmon to get the virus. Oddly enough, he says it doesn't happen to humans, or even eagles and vultures.

Eventually my social life improved. I was eager to be flying again, so I checked out the Medford Airport. It was an opportune time. A group of twenty had just started a non-profit corporation and bought a new Piper J3 with a 50–horsepower Franklin engine. As a member I would be able to fly for less than half the cost of renting the plane. I joined on the spot. I had my wings again. Because of the Depression, private flying had almost stopped, and the larger planes were too expensive to buy and maintain. Now, once again there were several smaller, light planes available, the top three being the Piper Cub, the Taylorcraft, and the Aeronca. By now they all had 50–horsepower engines, and that extra ten horsepower made the world of difference. A new light plane cost about one and a half times the price of a new Ford, Chevy, or Dodge.

It was a revolutionary time for aviation. The Model T Ford put America on wheels, and the light planes were giving the gift of flying to thousands. Cars had never meant more to me than a necessary means of transportation, but an airplane was a different story. It gave me the chance to see the world from above in a way I'd never dreamed possible. It also saved time. It could fly in a straight line, getting me where I wanted to go in half the time it would have taken me to wind around the mountain roads to the same place. The biggest problem was the lack of landing strips. On the other hand, small planes didn't need such a large field. I'd come to aviation at the right time.

I continued to make bridle bits for Porters, and now that I had the correct tools and more experience, I could turn them out much faster than before. I also got a new customer: The Charlie Reed Saddlery in Klamath Falls, Oregon. Reed's saddle shop was small, but he maintained a good business from the many cattle ranches in the area. Times were better now, too, so I raised my prices, which finally put me in the clear. I was even managing to save some money.

Christmas and New Years holidays were difficult for me. I was virtually alone. There were no Christmas cards, no invitations, and no one really to celebrate with. It was New Years that hit me the hardest. "Auld Lang Syne" had always been a favorite of mine. For everyone else, it seemed, it meant getting together, holding hands, and singing—something I'd never done in all my twenty-eight years. Normally I was content to be alone, but there was something about that season that got me feeling sorry for myself. I knew it was my own fault, but that didn't make the ache go away. Horses used to be enough for me, but that was before I spent time in Phoenix. Powder was with me, but she wasn't enough to keep the holidays from being overwhelmed with sadness. I turned to a bottle of Canadian Monogram Rye Whiskey for company on those lonely nights. I only drank at night, so by morning it was over. No regrets, no apologies to make to myself.

In the spring all I could think of was buying my own plane, but I'd need a field to fly from. Old Ferry Road was on about a quarter mile of flat ground that ended by the river below my house. Since I was the only one using the road, it seemed like the perfect place for landing. The county road commissioner gave me a permit, but only as long as I maintained the road. He also gave me an abandoned small horse-drawn grader the county no longer used, and with that I smoothed out a good runway. Unfortunately, like Fram's field in Arizona, because of the tall trees, it required a turn after take-off and again before landing. I practiced on my new field with the club's plane before taking the bus to Portland to look at a new Cub. Art Whittaker, the Piper dealer and distributor, was on Swan Island. So was my plane—a new Piper J3 Sport. That was Sunday, June 19.

All I needed now was a hangar. Back to Mr. Bristow. With his help and my design, it didn't take us long. Rough lumber was inexpensive, and there was a new sawmill right here in Shady Cove. I wanted a dirt floor. I got a fifty-foot piece of steel cable to support the front span and eight by twelve timbers for the ends. I wanted forty feet of doors across the front. I'd never seen this done, but I didn't see why it wouldn't work. We built the doors of lightweight wood and hinged them on the bottom to a long double beam dug in below ground level. That way the doors could be lowered to lie flat and latch together. Since the plane only weighed six hundred pounds, I could easily pull it in or out over the doors. Because of the space, air resistance underneath allowed the doors to go down gently.

I loved the rhythm in my life. I'd work until late afternoon and then fly for an hour or so. My next goal was to get my private license so I could take others up with me. So far Powder had been my only passenger. I was teaching myself to read maps, and I was navigating more or less by compass, flying to every field within an hour's reach. Since most compasses in light planes were notoriously inaccurate then, it was safer to navigate by reading the sectional and regional maps. The mountainous area made it confusing, as well as dangerous. I found the higher I flew, the easier it was. If I flew low, I followed the highway or the famous "Iron Compass"—railroad tracks. The only other way was by radio beams, and they were only used by the airlines and some of the expensive planes. Also, the receivers were high-priced.

I practiced all the maneuvers I'd need for the license: stalls, spins, and simulated forced landings. We all knew that the instructors giving the test would suddenly close the throttle, and the pilots were expected to find a field, glide down, and approach it until we were about fifteen feet above the ground. When it was obvious we could make a safe landing, he'd open the throttle and we'd fly it back up. The spins were done solo while the instructors watched from the ground. During one of my practice sessions, I landed in Klamath Falls in winds stronger than I'd ever faced before. I was coming in into the wind, and just as I was about to make a good three-point landing, I found myself flying slowly *backwards*. In fact, that's how I landed—backwards. I taxied up to the gas pumps where the operator, an older retired Navy pilot, asked why I hadn't made a wheel landing. I haven't any idea how, I told him. "Would you like me to show you how?" he asked. Indeed I did. And he did. I offered to pay him, but he wouldn't hear of it.

On July 6 I took my test in Eugene. I passed the written test easily, but when I met with the instructor I'd drawn, I wasn't so confident. Rubert Herr was a retired Navy pilot and the one man everyone dreaded taking the flight exam with. Everyone swore they'd never even seen the man smile. When the test was over, he motioned for me to sit down. "You flew well enough," he said, "but I've seen the landing strip you fly out of. I've flown over it several times, and I think it's an unsafe runway. However, I'll give you your license if you give me your word you'll never fly out of there with a passenger." With a big sigh of relief, I gave him my word.

Actually, fog seemed a lot more dangerous to me than my field. Fog has always been a problem for flying in the winter in my area. Sometimes we'd be socked in for weeks at a time. Around 1939 United Airlines made only one trip a day from Seattle or Portland to Los Angeles with a stopover in Medford. If the fog was bad in Medford, they couldn't land there. I knew a man who never liked the idea of flying but got talked into it when he was in a hurry to get to a meeting in Portland the following day. When the plane got to Portland, the field was socked in, so the plane went on to Seattle. He missed his meeting and had to spend the night in Seattle. The next day he took a flight back to Medford, only Medford was socked in and they flew on to San Francisco. That airport was also fogged in, so the plane continued on to Los Angeles, where he had to spend the night. The next day Medford airport was still closed, so they flew him to San Francisco and gave him a free ticket on the Greyhound bus to Medford.

Planes and cars were not my only means of transportation. From May to October, I swam across the river to get my mail. On my return trip, I'd hold the mail between my teeth while I did the backstroke. During the winter months I'd drive the two miles around. Finally, I bought a used old surplus Navy inflatable one-man raft. That was a lot easier than swimming, though I had some wild rides.

My plane gave me a way to make a little extra money. Bristow had the lower part of the land planted in strawberries, asparagus, and grape vines. Since I had no intention of gardening, I let Bristow continue to raise his crops there for several years. Sometimes I'd pick an entire crate of strawberries and fly them to Charlie at the saddle shop in Klamath Falls. There a cup of strawberries sold for what Bristow got for the whole crate.

I had a strange and unexpected visitor at my shop one day— an Oregon state policeman asking a string of questions: *Did I go fishing? Was I a hunter? Why did I fly a plane? What was I making in the shop?* He was remarkably overweight for a policeman. I couldn't figure what this was all about. I showed him what I was making and how. That instigated another series of questions: *Was I using real silver? Where did I get it? How much did it cost?* After awhile I quit working, sat down on the anvil, and listened to him jabber on until he finally wore down. The man hadn't made any sense, and neither did his visit.

Not long after that a teller at our local bank asked in a whisper if I knew I was being investigated. Apparently, the FBI and local officials both had been in the bank checking my accounts. I knew I hadn't done anything illegal, so this was upsetting. It was another month before the mystery was solved. It was on the front page of our local paper: "Counterfeiter arrested in Gold Hill." The strange thing is that the counterfeit silver dollars contained no silver at all. They were cast from babbitt metal, a lead-tin alloy heavier than silver used mostly for bearings in all types of machinery. I'd never heard of anyone foolish enough to try to use it for counterfeit money.

Several months after the encounter with the Oregon policeman, I had a meeting much more to my liking. I met a policeman at the airport who said he wished the police had another plane to use to search for missing people, because the local operator was charging them too much for their limited budget. I needed to build up my flying time, so I offered to help them out at no charge. Not long after that I was able to spot two missing children. They were happily picking flowers about a quarter of a mile away from the riverbank. Another time, I was asked to search for a fourteen-year-old boy who'd argued with his father the night before and then disappeared. It took only ten minutes to spot him walking along a logging railroad.

I was no longer leading the lonely life I'd led for so long. One thing kept leading to another. One day I flew over to Roseburg, a small city about sixty-five miles to the north. There was a good landing strip close to town. I no sooner, landed when about a dozen cars pulled over and stopped. People tumbled out and ran over to look at my plane. Roseburg, I learned, had no operator at the landing strip, but there were many folks interested in flying. I was there at least an hour answering their questions. They begged me to find an operator for them. A Stinson, owned by a local mill worker, was the only private plane at the field.

I returned a couple of days later and asked if an operator with one or two planes could make a living there. "We can keep him busy from daylight to dark," was their answer. I knew just the person for them—Red Sink. I airmailed a letter to him in Phoenix, and heard back immediately. Indeed, he was interested, and as luck would have it, he'd just gotten a dealership for a new light airplane, the Welch OW, named after the designer Otis Welch. Red flew to my place a few days later. We stayed up most of night talking airplanes and hatching a plan.

The next day we flew over Roseburg. The plan was for me to fly to the west while Red flew to the east for about a quarter of a mile. We then headed back past each other and we both went over in a loop. We looped again, and then we each did a hammerhead stall, followed by a spin. By the time we landed, I bet there were a hundred cars heading our way. We offered rides for a dollar and made out very well. It had been a huge success, and we were feeling mighty good until a worried looking man approached us. "Please don't fly over, or even near, that group of large red brick buildings southwest of your landing strip," he said. "Those buildings are US Army Hospital wards for the mentally ill veterans. We've already tied down and sedated twenty-eight men from the trauma of hearing your planes." Red and I felt awful, but really there was no way we could have known. We'd seen no signs and it wasn't shown on our aerial map, as it should have been. Red did start a flying club there and ran it for several years.

Mr. Herr, the frozen-face, grumpy Civil Aviation Authority inspector who tested me in Eugene, showed up at the Medford Airport one day and beckoned me over. Before he opened his mouth, I said, "I've never ever taken a passenger in or out of my field." He *almost* smiled, then only nodded and asked what I was going to do with my flying career. I told him I just enjoyed flying and I looked forward to being better and better at it. "Have you considered becoming a flight instructor?" he asked. "Aviation is growing so fast that there's a critical shortage of good instructors."

I was honored at his suggestion, but I had to tell him about my poor scholastic record, adding that if he could suggest books, I'd learn what I had to learn on my own. He gave me two of his own books and some pamphlets on the Civil Air Regulations to study. I was staggered by it all, but I decided to go for it.

Not a day went by that I didn't spend hours pouring over those books. Aerial flight navigation is different from the flight navigation as taught to and by Navy pilots. The problems were much the same, but with different figures. A typical problem might be this: You were to take off from aircraft carrier A and fly to carrier B, and land. You knew the given speeds, the direction of the carriers, and the wind direction. You also knew that when you landed on carrier B it would keep moving. At a given time, you'd fly back and land on carrier A, which had been moving all this time and maybe on a different course. The wind may have changed by now as well. So how were you going to get back to the carrier you took off from? This was not going to be easy.

I bought a protractor, a few other tools, and a roll of butcher paper. I smoothed out a place on the floor where I could roll out a two-foot square, and I got to work. It was sheer hell for the first few days until I gradually began to catch on. It took me a couple of weeks to understand and work out the problems, though. I'd never worked with degrees, and compass declination was another factor I had to reckon with. I was my own teacher and my own worst critic. In the end, though, it made everything else much easier because the CAA (Civil Aviation Authority, now the Federal Aviation Authority) exams focused on land-based fields and airports. *They didn't move.* The wind and compass variations were the only variables I had to work with.

As for the compasses—the nearly useless compasses in those light planes were what caused pilots the most trouble during those years. They were made inexpensively and couldn't be trusted within twenty or thirty degrees. Another problem was that some of the engines in the planes were so bad and so rough that they caused the instruments to fail. I remember a new plane that was flown out from the factory, and by the time it landed in Portland all of the instruments were broken except the nearly worthless compass. I flew a plane once with an engine that had a reputation for losing its needles in flight. That was scary, since we usually flew IFR then, which meant: *I Follow Railroads*, not Instrument Flight Regulations.

Civil Pilot Training (CPT) programs were growing quickly, but they were only available to college students with good grades and students willing to make themselves available to the Navy as volunteers after completing three stages. The first stage was the equivalent of a private license. The second stage was considerably more advanced, requiring all the aerobatic maneuvers the Navy taught in their pilot training program. The third stage was the cross-country trip from Medford to Redding, California, from Redding to Klamath Falls, and then back to Medford. All students who passed the second stage had forty-eight hours to report to the nearest Navy recruiting depot. Obviously, this wasn't a free ride.

The first stage could be taught in light airplanes, but the second had to be taught in fully aerobatic and licensed planes, of which there were very few at the time. I realized I could probably sell my plane to the program for a good price. I loved my Cub #23297, but they were now making them with 60–horsepower engines, and for what I wanted to do, the extra ten horsepower would be good. The factories making light planes could hardly keep up with the orders, so I knew it could take awhile until I'd get one. I called Art Whitaker and asked for help. No problem. If I'd be willing to go to the factory and fly it out, I could get it fairly quickly. I was willing.

I sold my Cub to Tom Culbertson, the operator at the Medford Airport and the man who ran the CPT program there. Then I met Silas King in Portland, and the two of us took a Greyhound bus to State College, Pennsylvania—five long days and nights bouncing around. From State College we flew in a small eight-passenger plane to Lock Haven.

The Cub factory was housed in a long building beside a platform about twelve feet above the ground. Each time a new plane was to be tested, it was rolled out onto this platform, filled with a gallon or so of gas, and started up. Kenny Kress, the test pilot, would fly the plane off the ramp, over the highway and power lines, and land on the field across the street. On the take-off one wing tip was only a foot or so from the side of the building. The other wing was out over the railroad tracks, and the outer wheel was less than two inches from the edge. Kenny was good.

I was excited when they agreed to check me out in one of the new experimental models—the three-place Cub Cruiser with a 75–horsepower Lycoming engine. I was even more excited on the third day when our planes were ready. Silas's plane was a Cub coupe with side-by-side seating. Mine was a Sport Monoplane with a 60–horsepower engine. Brakes were an available option, but absolutely essential for the short fields I flew in and out of, so when I saw my plane had no brakes, I refused to sign for it. Despite the fact that my order form proved the brakes had been ordered and paid for, they gave me a hard time, even going so far as to say they had none available at the time. That did it! I could see a pair on a used factory plane not fifty feet away. I told them I'd spent five days and nights on a lousy bus and I didn't plan to leave without my plane and its brakes, even if it meant suing them. In a huff they pulled my plane back in. Thirty minutes later it had brakes.

Lock Haven is in a valley with the Susquehanna River running through it and mountains on the west side. We were determined to get over those mountains before dark, so Silas and I left in a hurry. We spent the first night in Dubois, Pennsylvania. The following day we made three stops to refill: one at Youngstown, Ohio, one at Fort Wayne, Indiana, and then at Davenport, Iowa.

My Cub Sport had a smaller gas tank than Silas's Coupe, but Whittaker had loaned me a device he'd invented that allowed me two extra hours of flying time—an auxiliary aluminum gas tank with a small, built-in wobble pump and a rubber hose stored in a side pocket of its case, which looked like a leather suitcase. Since the Cub Sport was flown solo from the rear seat, it was easy to strap the tank to the front seat. The hose went under the corner of the windshield to a special gas cap with a fitting to take the hose. Because it was illegal, it had to be disguised. I marveled at the beauty of our country as it passed under my wings. Chicago had looked so filthy from the Greyhound, but from the air it was lovely against the blue lake and the white sails on the small boats. I was amazed to see the uniformity of the farmer's fields.

From Davenport we flew to Cheyenne, Wyoming. The next morning we flew to Pocatello, Idaho, stopping only to gas up at

Rock Springs. After we passed over the continental divide, we had to change course sharply to the right to get to Bear Lake, our next gas stop. Silas was leading, since his plane was faster. He was to keep an eye on me, so I was surprised when he neglected to make that sharp turn. Several miles past that point, he began a slow left turn. That gave me an advantage. I cut straight across to get close to him. I'd figured he must have fallen asleep. I was right. Just then, he quickly turned to the right in a steep turn and kept on until he spotted me again. The experience scared him to death. He told me later he had no idea how long he'd been asleep. I suspect it was only for about three minutes or so.

In the midst of all this, I had a mishap myself. The hose came off the wobble pump and the gas squirted directly in my face. Luckily it missed my eyes, but it found my mouth with perfect aim. I had to open the side door and vomit it out. I was still feeling pretty sick when we landed in Bear Lake.

We spent that night in Bear Lake, then flew on to The Dalles the next morning. By the time we started down the Columbia River, the wind was so strong and picking up that we couldn't make much headway. We barely got to Hood River, a small city on the south shore, and then a mile past that we found ourselves being blown backwards. After another thirty minutes of that, we headed back to The Dalles Airport, thankful that we'd filled up at John Day. Because there was no one there, we had to sit in our planes for two hours, keeping then running so they'd stay in one place until someone finally came to help us tie them down. A little before dark the wind died down and we made it to Swan Island. I flew home to Shady Cove the next day.

My sights were firmly set on becoming an instructor. I knew it had to be a good job for me. So many people wanted to learn to fly and buying a plane was now within their financial reach. In the meantime, when the Medford Airport local operator asked if I'd like to demonstrate a new plane for him, I readily accepted. He had just gotten the dealership for a new and radically different small plane with side-to-side seating—a low-wing monoplane with retractable landing gear and a 75–horsepower engine that could cruise at a hundred and ten miles an hour. My first assignment was to fly up to John Day and demonstrate the plane for a doctor who was considering purchasing one. The minute I saw him, I knew it would never be a sale. He knew it, too. The man had to weigh at least two hundred pounds. He looked at the plane, grinned, and said, "If I can squeeze in, will you give me a ride?" I had to rearrange the seats and share half of my seat with him, but somehow we managed. Of course, he didn't buy the plane.

Too many people were buying and renting planes and flying when they weren't qualified. There was a fatal plane crash west of Shady Cove involving two Army lieutenants in charge of a CCC camp beside an unused grain field. One of them had rented an old Cub trainer from the Grants Pass Airport, flown it back, and landed on the grain field to pick up the other officer. They took off toward the east, where there was a tall ponderosa pine at the far side of the field. Without any turns or maneuvers, the plane had flown straight into that tree at about sixty feet. Neither man had a solo permit. The CAA verified that neither had ever applied for a license, nor did they have a CAA certificate, a basic requirement to fly a particular plane before renting it.

I got a call from the *Air Facts* magazine asking me to inspect the site and gather as much information as I could about the accident. This magazine was a small but good publication that reviewed all new airplanes intended to be used by the general public. They also reviewed accidents, in the hope of preventing others. I found no error in the takeoff. The only possible cause of the accident was that the officer sitting in front of the pilot had blocked his view.

A few months later the same man who'd rented the plane to the lieutenants sold an old biplane he'd advertised as being licensed and in good condition. Neither were true. The young man from eastern Oregon who bought the plane had just flown over the Cascade Mountains, when all the fabric came off the wings. It cost him his life.

October 23 was a day to remember. I got my commercial license. A few months later I was given a 2-S rating, which allowed me to fly for-hire planes up to 500-horsepower. Now I could earn real money at the Medford Airport. My first class of CPT primary students consisted of one woman and nine men (which was the requirement: one woman for every nine men). I taught them in the Cubs, often using the Cub 23297 I'd sold to the program.

Now that I was qualified to fly a number of different planes, flying became even more enjoyable. I flew the stable and comfortable four-place Fairchild 24 with a 145–horsepower Warner engine. I also flew a Waco Cabin biplane with a 225–horsepower Jacobs engine, a radio receiver, and fine instruments. The only problem with some of the Wacos is that their wheels were fairly close together, which made them hard to handle without ground-looping or nosing over. At that time all planes had conventional landing gear—two main wheels in front and a small tail wheel behind. In landing, the pilot would slow the plane down until it settled on the runway on all three wheels at the same time. He then kept it rolling straight ahead as it slowed down even more. If there was a crosswind and the plane landed drifting sideways, the tail would snap around in a tightening spiral and the plane would sometimes wind up on its nose. If it landed with the tail in the air, the propeller would be ruined. Because of this, most three-to-four- passenger planes had the wheels set fairly far apart.

I frequently flew the two-place Waco UPF7 aerobatic biplane. Its landing gear was wider, and it had a locking tailwheel that I could lock in the center to keep it straight on landing. But I chose the Waco Cabin for charter flights, as it was faster and easier getting in and out of shorter fields. I just had to watch it on landing. A disadvantage to the Waco Cabin was that it had a lever about a foot long down near the center of the cockpit. It was used to apply the brakes. Most planes had foot brakes operated by either pressing on top of the rudder pedals or having heel brakes to the side of the pedals. In this Waco I had to reach down, which wouldn't have been such a problem, except that the plane had a half wheel, or yoke, instead of a control stick, and the throttle was set in the center of the panel. This made for a serious problem because I couldn't use the brakes and the throttle at the same time since both required the use of my right hand. I flew a US senator to Eureka one day, and in an emergency situation, when he didn't get his leg out of the way in time, I grabbed his leg when I reached for the brake. Apparently, my fingernails had dug in pretty deep.

Because I spent so much time at the airport, I began staying nights in boarding houses in Medford and eating in restaurants instead of doing my own cooking at home. But that's how I finally found out who that obese policeman was who'd popped into my shop a while back. I got to know an Oregon state policeman, as we both ate in the same restaurants, and I asked if he knew anything about that man. He said the man had been forced on the police department through a political move. He was a burden to the police, but there wasn't a thing they could do about it. Eventually, he was caught having sold a .30-.30 rifle he'd stolen from the evidence room. I ran into that ex-policeman a year or so later, but this time he was wearing greasy, oil-covered overalls and working at an airport.

My friend Denton offered to share his new three-bedroom apartment in Medford with me. That was great. No more boarding houses. The only drawback was the location. Denton was our new county jailer, and his quarters were on the third floor of the building—the same floor as the jail. We had some interesting and exciting experiences, but the one that scared me the most was the time the policemen asked if I'd like to see one of the most vicious criminals they'd ever caught. Always curious, of course I said yes. They opened the door to a large room that held the man's cell. As soon as I entered they slammed the door shut. I heard a loud pop, and something they'd thrown in with me started to smoke. Let me tell you, I screamed and yelled and banged on that door. I had just been their first guinea pig to be tested with a device to be thrown into a building to force a criminal out.

When it was too foggy to fly, I'd stay at the apartment with Denton, but most days I was too busy to take a break. Students were always lined up and waiting. I'd tell them good pilots flew ninety-eight percent with their head and two perecent with their hands and feet, excluding takeoffs and landings. A properly rigged plane will fly itself with only minor corrections. Many problems were caused by the show-off syndrome. Too many young people crashed right in front of the people they wanted to impress.

There were several times when I went to the CAA to get a permit for someone physically unfit by their standards. I'll never forget a thirty-year-old man who'd been obsessed with planes since he was a young boy. He always showed up wearing light gloves, but I didn't think much about it. After he'd soloed perfectly, he removed his left glove to reveal an artificial left hand and asked me if

I'd go to bat for him with the CAA. Now that Rupert Herr had been replaced by Ed Teach, a friend of mine, I thought he had a fighting chance. Nevertheless, I didn't say a word until after he'd passed his exam for his private license. Ed flew with him and had to admit that he was an excellent pilot. Ed agreed that as long as he wore gloves no one would know the difference.

The most money I made in a day then was the time a storm devastated much of the West Coast and a large coastal steamer went ashore near Coos Bay. Two photographers representing the insurance company flew into Medford from New York and needed to get to Coos Bay. The weather was still unsettled and I knew that the landing strip was just above the shoreline, but I agreed to take them. I won't risk my neck though, I told them. As was customary, they paid for the charter before we took off. I flew the Fairchild 24, as it landed slower and was an excellent plane. Its cruising speed was only a hundred and twenty miles per hour, but Coos Bay was only a little over a hundred miles away. They loaded their gear in the baggage compartment behind the rear seat and climbed in the two passenger seats in tandem. Because of the weather, I flew con-siderably north until I found a pass to get over the Coastal Moun-tain Range, then down the coast to Coos Bay. The landing strip was totally under water. I kept circling, keeping my eye on a fence post on one side of the field to determine the depth of the water. After twenty minutes we all agreed to chance it. Knowing the big-gest danger would be in nosing over when the wheels hit the water, I had the man up front climb in the back. The men were so grateful to have landed safely that, as they jumped out in knee-deep water, one of them handed me a twenty dollar bill. That was equivalent to a hundred dollars today. I spent the rest of the day showing it off to everyone at the Medford Airport.

I had an encounter that didn't mean much to me at the time, but a year later it did. One evening a Rearwin Sportster landed at Medford. "Robert Crawford—the Flying Baritone" was printed on the side of the plane. The following morning when the fog pre-vented us from flying, I saw Crawford writing on a portable music stand. When I asked what he was doing, he politely replied that the Army has "And the Caissons Keep Rolling Along," the Navy has "Anchors Aweigh," but the Army Air Corps had no song of its own.

He intended to give them one. "Can you sing?" he asked me. "Definitely not," I told him. "Can you hum?" he asked. I said I could try, and that's how I got to be the first person ever to hear and hum along with the first stanza of "Off We Go Into the Wild Blue Yonder." We worked on that song until noon, when the fog lifted and I had to fly.

A year later, I read that Major Robert Crawford was in command of the Army Air Corps Band, and, yes the Army Air Corps had its own song now.

Military planes were landing and refueling in Medford on a steady basis now. The Army Air Corps' main fighter plane was the P-40, a low-wing monoplane with an Allison engine, an engine that had earned itself a bad reputation. One morning as I was taxiing out with a student, we had to wait until a P-40 took off. By the time we were prepared to takeoff, the sky had darkened and that P-40 came in not ten feet over us with a dead engine. The landing gear was retracted, wheels up out of sight in the belly. He went about a hundred feet and landed on the dirt instead of the paved runway. The plane had a sort of inverted hump on the bottom of the fuselage. It hit the dirt going about ninety miles an hour and spun like a top. It spun over and over in a cloud of dust before slowing down. I jumped out and ran over, but just as I reached the plane, the pilot threw open the cockpit and jumped out on the wing. He fell off and rolled onto the ground. He tried to stand up, but he couldn't make it. His eyes were spinning around and around. I stayed with him until the crash wagon arrived. He was a remarkable young man. He'd taken off, turned south to return to his base in San Francisco, and then, just as he reached two thousand feet over Medford, the engine blew up. Since the controls were still working, and since he knew the plane would surely hit some houses if he ditched it, he chose to attempt a landing. As it was, the entire armor plate and the bottom of the engine landed in the street by a bakery. Although it was a busy street, no one was injured. About a year later a student of mine was killed in a P-40 when the engine blew up.

I've kept my log book all these years, so I know what dates and kinds of planes I was flying, but I was stumped about ten or twelve years ago when I answered the phone and a voice said, "Is this Tom Tepper? I'll give you five hundred guesses and you still won't guess who I am." I said I probably would if I could ask a few questions. None of my questions led me to the answer. Finally he said, "I'll give you a clue: Slow rolls with the sun as the axis."

"Billy Plasket!" I yelled. Billy had been my gas boy years ago, and he took his pay in flying lessons. Occasionally I'd take him up in the Waco biplane, the one I used for aerobatic maneuvers. I'd flown enough with him in the Cub that I knew he could easily have soloed, but he wasn't yet sixteen. We did slow rolls using the sun, which was just beginning to show, as the axis point, and then we'd roll it three hundred and sixty degrees until it came back to level.

"If I live to be a thousand," he told me on that phone that night, "I'll never forget what an experience that was. I've just retired as senior captain after twenty-six years with Western Airlines. I'm in Medford waiting for a flight, and I thought maybe I could find you in the phone book."

Those are the memories worth holding on to. I have sad memories, too, lots of them. I got a call once from a man just across the border in California. Said he had to get to San Francisco that day. I flew down in the Fairchild and picked up a man in his fifties. He pulled a photograph from his pocket and asked if I'd ever seen her. I hadn't. The poor soul was a mail carrier and had been a bachelor for years. The only thing he did for entertainment was to go to the local Saturday night dances. He was so innocent that when a woman professed her love for him after only a few dances, he fell for it and her. He took her home with him and the next morning he proposed. She readily accepted. After they were married, he foolishly bought a new Cadillac, put both of their names on the title and went off to work. When he came home, she and the car were both gone. His checkbook was gone as well. He had some money cached away, though, and he'd pay me with that, he said.

San Francisco was where she'd told him she was from, so that's where he figured she'd return to. He reported the stolen car and checkbook to both police stations, and in each he was told. "If it's your wife who took it, she has as much right to it as you do. There's nothing we can do about it." We spent the night in some cheap hotel, though he would have preferred to walk the streets all night looking for her. The next day he insisted I stop in Sacramento. The sergeant there told him he might as well go home and forget about it. I took him home, but I doubt very much that he ever forgot about it.

As a pilot, one is never finished learning. I passed a simple test through the CAA enabling me to teach Civil Air Regulations and basic meteorology. That knowledge came in handy both for me and my students many times throughout the years. I met a meteorologist in the weather bureau in the Bay Area, but we weren't able to converse much, since he could barely talk at all. He'd been one of the original pilots for Pacific Air Transport, now United Airlines. Those brave pilots were flying biplanes with the old early engines and no navigational aids except for a compass and an altimeter. Airways and beacons (towers with strong rotating lights that turned on automatically at dark and stayed on until daylight) were unknown at the time. These pilots followed Highway 99 from Seattle to Los Angeles. They called themselves the PATS (Pacific Air Transport Skullduggers). This meteorologist had been flying with four passengers from California to Portland when he got into bad weather and hit a mountain north of Medford. He had pulled his four dead passengers out of the crushed and burned cabin even though he was badly burned himself. He lost most of his fingers, nose and lips, and virtually had no face left. He dedicated the rest of his life to navigational aids.

I'm grateful to him and to all of those brave men who pioneered in aviation. I eventually got considerable experience in instrument flying, but most of us here in the mountains know that in a single-engine plane you can't count on instruments alone. They won't save you if your engine fails. We had an old saying that's still applicable today: "Through stormy weather he swore he'd get. Ten years have passed. He ain't here yet."

A perfect example of that happened when Dick, a member of the Medford Flying Club, showed up at the field with his wife. He planned on flying the club plane to Portland. The fog was so thick you couldn't see the end of the runway. Even United shut down. When he was told it was impossible, he pulled out his little radio receiver capable of receiving the same radio beams the airlines used. We all knew they were almost useless as navigational aids. The mechanic winked at me and left for a few minutes. When he returned, he said the battery was in town being recharged. That didn't stop Dick. He simply went into town, bought a new battery for the plane and prepared to leave. His wife, already scared to death of flying under any conditions, was a nervous wreck. I remember her pulling on a pair of black gloves just before they took off under the fog layer ten feet above the ground.

Because they hadn't filed a flight plan, no immediate search was ordered when friends of theirs in Portland called to ask friends in Medford where they were. Eventually, the CAA listed them as missing and began a search, but by then it was November and the weather made the search very difficult. Eleven years later, October 1951, a friend of mine was deer hunting on Mt. Bailey, an eight thousand-foot mountain ninety miles northeast of Medford. He spotted a lady's black shoe and when he picked it up, toe bones fell out. He looked around and found two wheels and tires sticking out above the low brush. It was the Medford Flying Club plane. There were two skulls inside.

In September,1941 Art Whittaker offered me a job I accepted immediately. I became the traveling representative covering Washington, Oregon, and Idaho for Whittaker, who was the sole distributor for Piper, Cessna, and Bellanca airplanes. My new job certainly improved my navigation skills. I had to find my way over brand new territory, including many of the high, snow-capped mountains. I no longer had any routine to my life, though, and I was forced to skip too many meals. I was demonstrating three planes to as many possible buyers as I could, and since people who have the flying bug will go to their local airport whenever they can regardless of the hour, my time was no longer my own. Most airports were far from town, and few of them had anything to eat except for Coke and candy machines. Coke and peanuts became my usual dinner.

Other than that, I loved my job, especially the surprise sales. Like the time in Bend when I demonstrated a new Cub Sport to a man who arrived just before dark. After I gave him a ride, I headed to the Pilot Butte Inn for dinner, only it was closed. I bought another Coke and a couple of packs of Planters and went to my room. There I was lying on the bed, Coke in one hand and peanuts in the other, when someone knocked on the door. It was the last man I'd flown. All he said was, "I'd like to buy one. How soon can I get it?" If only all sales were that easy!

I had a close call that fall with an Army twin-engine Martin bomber. These pilots based in Boise, Idaho usually flew their missions very high, but this day I was flying across the semi-desert country in eastern Washington at about five thousand feet. As I did sometimes when I was far away from air traffic, I was reading an aviation magazine and looking up every now and then to stay on course. This time I looked up right into the face of a young man in the clear plastic machine gunner's pod in the nose of the bomber about two hundred feet ahead. I pulled the throttle and prayed I'd judged correctly—that we'd pass and I'd go under his wing. In a second it was over, but I'll never forget the young flyer's expression with his mouth wide open. Guess he's saying the same about me.

I made two unsuccessful trips to Aberdeen, Washington trying to contact a man who'd expressed interest in a Piper dealership. On the way home I turned on my portable radio, and all I could get was a man shouting so excitedly that I couldn't catch a word he was saying. I switched to another station and got the same thing. I tried another and all I could make out was a sound like "Pullhobba, Pulhobba." Then clearly, "The Japanese have attacked." I'd never heard of "Pullhobba" but I knew this was no joke. I headed straight for the nearest town and stopped at a service station. There, huddled over a map, was a group of people looking for Pearl Harbor. When I fully realized what had happened and where, I drove as fast as I could to Swan Island off the coast of Portland, where Art Whittaker and Silas King were now working. Silas and Art were extremely upset. They had just gotten word that all planes were grounded, except for the airlines and the military. That was December 7, 1941. We were in shock. Whittaker had me fly the Eaglerock across the river to Vancouver and put it in a hangar. When I got back, he filled three glasses of Coke and added a big shot of bourbon to each. It didn't make us feel any better. The big question was: What in the world should we do next? I knew what I had to do. I had no family, so there was no reason for me not to volunteer.

Just then the CAA called again saying there were rumors that the Japanese might attack the West Coast, or possibly they had spies already in place capable of blowing up the bridges. Whittaker was to post armed guards starting at six that night to protect the airport on Swan Island. I was handed a barely serviceable Colt .38

revolver with six tarnished, old cartridges in it. Then I just waited around until dark. A further radio announcement ordered the entire city blacked out, including car lights and electric signs. The only bit of humor that night was the large sign with a huge man holding a frying pan, bending over a fire and flipping a flapjack in the air. This repeated itself every minute throughout the night. For some reason that sign was never turned off, and that was all you could see of that night.

At dark I went to defend Swan Island. I had a partner—a young fellow who was extremely slow and extremely scared. I was to guard the south side of the island (Swan Island is actually a long, narrow peninsula with only one road in or out), and my counterpart was to take the north end. Ten-foot cherry trees surrounded the island, making it difficult to see the river normally, but tonight it was also pitch black. I had to wait at least fifteen minutes for my partner to get to the checkpoint on our trip around, and on the second, just before I reached the checkpoint, he jumped out and hollered, "Freeze!" He was not five feet from me, aiming his gun at my stomach. He was shaking like a leaf. I didn't feel so calm myself. Once I'd finished my ranting and threatening him if he did that again, we agreed he would sing out each time we got close from then on.

Our relief came at two A.M. I slept in my car until daylight, and then drove to the nearest Army recruiting station in Portland. The line was a block and a half long already. When I finally got to the desk and told them I was a commercial pilot, they sent me to Pierson Field in Vancouver to see the commanding officer. I found the officer sitting on the steps outside his office hand-feeding some bantam chickens. He looked up and said quietly, "We should have been more prepared. Right now the total number of qualified Army Air Corps pilots ready for action in the category they were trained for is twenty-eight hundred. I doubt they have that many new planes either, but don't repeat these numbers," he warned. He looked at my logbooks and said that with my rating I could do the greatest service by becoming an instructor at one of the Army Air Corps training schools. I promised to do just that.

Chapter 12

The Army Air Corps

HIGH FLIGHT
Oh! I have slipped the surly bonds of earth
And danced the skies on laughter-silvered wings:
Sunward I've climbed, and joined the tumbling mirth
Of sun-split clouds—and done a hundred things
You have not dreamed of—wheeled and soared and swung
High in the sun-lit silence. Hov'ring there, 0
I've chased the shouting wind along, and flung
My eager craft through footless halls of air.
Up, up, the delirious burning blue
I've topped the wind-swept heights with easy grace
Where never lark or even eagle flew—
And, while with silent lifting mind I've trod
The high untresspassed sanctity of space,
Put out my hand and touched the face of God.
                    By John Gillespie Magee, Jr.
                    W.W. II Aviation Cadet

A couple of months before the bombing
of Pearl Harbor, I'd been offered a job as a flight instructor by the
US Marines and also the Cal Aero Flying Service. I hadn't responded
to either of them at the time, but now Cal Aero looked like a pos-
sibility. I packed my belongings in a suitcase, threw it in my '41
Chevy Coupe, and headed south. Having made all the arrangements
I needed to in Shady Cove, I then drove somewhere past Sacramento that night before stopping. In the morning I found myself
in Tulare, where Red Sink was instructing in an Air Corps Train-

ing Center. I decided to drop by and say hello. That was a stroke of luck. Red introduced me to Tex Rankin, the world champion aerobatic pilot I'd seen fly in Phoenix. When Tex asked to have a look at my logbook, I was honored, and when he told me I was needed right there with him, it wasn't difficult to persuade me to stay. This place had a reputation as the best of all Air Corps primary schools, and to be with a man like Tex Rankin was reason enough to stay. I signed up, and that was one decision I never regretted. Not only did I love what I was doing, but I loved being in the San Joaquin Valley, so close to the Sierras. It was also a pleasure to be close to all the many ranches, orange tree groves, and vineyards.

My flight test was given by Victor Torres in a Stearman, a two POLB, which means a two-place, open-land biplane, very similar to the Waco UPF I'd flown many times. Like the Waco, the Stearman had its wheels close together, which made it more difficult to land. That was the very reason it was an excellent plane for the students to learn on. If a student could fly and land this seventeen-thousand-dollar plane, he'd find it much easier to fly the more difficult and more expensive fighters when the time came.

After I was officially accepted, I rented a room in a quiet part of town. The next morning I was out at Rankin Field eager to get started. Torres gave me a tour of the place. Three hundred Stearmans were lined up and more expected. The roar of those 220–horsepower Continental engines could be heard from miles away. It was an excellent engine, though. Over the three years I was there, not one went down from engine failure, unless you count the one flown by an inept, know-it-all Army lieutenant.

That accident happened just before I arrived at Rankin. A lieutenant decided to prove that a placard on the panel in the cockpit with a red warning: **Do Not Hold Engine Between 1,500 and 1,700 RPMS** was unnecessary. He and a cadet took off for a one-hour flight, deliberately holding the RPM in the red zone. Fifty-five minutes later, while he was in the landing pattern, there was an explosion. A blade tore off the propeller, throwing it off balance and tearing the entire engine off. At five hundred feet, they were too low to parachute out. The plane came somersaulting down and hit the ground near the main gate. The lieutenant miraculously escaped with only bruises, but the cadet was flown to the hospital with serious jagged cuts around his eyes made by his broken goggles. It took more than two years for him to heal before he was able to return and graduate.

When I first arrived at Rankin, they were about thirty instructors short of full capacity. We were divided into eight flights of ten instructors. The flights were alphabetically named: Flight A, Flight B, Flight C, etc., and each of us was given five cadets. Howard Scheruer was my flight commander. With eighty instructors, forty of us flew in the morning, the other forty flew in the afternoon, rotating every other week. The differences between the CPT, Navy maneuvers, and the Army maneuvers were confusing to me at first, but I soon learned: *There is only one way—the Army way.* Many pilots came for refresher courses; some of the older pilots were the worst. They'd logged plenty of hours, but most of them had never done any aerobatics. They didn't believe in doing them, and they certainly didn't want to do them. Torres roped me into helping him teach these men.

Tulare had few restaurants, so I was trying them all. One evening a pretty, young girl took my order. I'd seen her before, but she'd never waited on me. This night they weren't busy, so when she brought my icecream float we talked a bit. Before leaving, I asked her for a date. Elva agreed to meet me at ten that night when she finished work.

For the first time in my life I fell in love. This was the woman I wanted to spend my life with. We were married in Visalia the last day of May in 1942. She honestly revolutionized my life. She deserves credit as much or more than I do for anything I've accomplished. Among other things, she has always handled all of our bookkeeping and finances. She worked physically beside me for many, long, hard hours, often all day and on into the night. I always tell Elva: "Beautiful and dumb my true love must be. Beautiful so I'll love her. Dumb so she'll love me."

According to Elva: Tom had been in the ice-cream parlor several times before he asked me for a date. I agreed to go out with him, and there he was waiting for me at three minutes before ten. I figured he'd have a little Model A, but instead he had a nice new '41 Chevy. We drove fifteen miles to buy some film and then he took me home. That was our date. The next day, we drove up in the mountains where there was snow. He wanted to take some pictures. Tom asked if I was engaged or anything. I told him if I was I wouldn't be there with him. A few days later Tom came in again. After he left, my boss asked why I hadn't charged him anything. "Because he didn't have anything," I said. "Do you think I'd give him something without charging him anything for it? That would be stealing from you, and if I did that to you, what do you think he would think of me? If that's what you think of me, I quit," I told him. And I did. I didn't even take the pay I had coming to me. Long about April we got engaged. We went to Fresno to get the ring. On the way home he pulled over in a patch of sunlight and gave it to me. Right before that he'd had me cook some stew for him. I guess he wanted to be sure I could cook before he gave me a ring. After we were married, we went to Visalia to a real nice restaurant for dinner. On the way home Tom stopped at a store for some bacon and eggs, bread, apple juice, and a can of soup. By the time we got home, he was hungry again, so I fixed the can of soup. That was our wedding day. Since we moved to Oregon in 1945, we've only eaten dinner out once, and Tom says that was a supreme sacrifice on his part. He said he'd eaten in restaurants so much when he was flying that he'd gotten to hating them. We used to eat lunch out now and then, though. Now, once a week, he wants to go to the Dairy Queen for a banana split and the one cup of coffee he has all week. He drinks tea, using the same bag over again and again as much as twelve times.

After our one-day honeymoon, I was back at Rankin taking my students up for their final check ride—done by another hard-nosed Army lieutenant we all hated to draw. One by one he took them up, and when the ride was finished, he simply walked away without a word. After the last one landed, this lieutenant marched into Howie Scheurer's office. A few minutes later he marched smartly back out. We were all holding our breath. What a relief it was when Howie came out grinning with good news. The lieutenant said all of my men had done difficult maneuvers, like the chandelle, better than any he'd seen a cadet do so far. We were all very proud. We had something else to be proud of too: not one of my cadets ever ground looped a plane.

One cadet from another flight made fame and history on his first flight. In the center of the home field was a large airplane-size

"T" mounted on a swivel base with an electric motor under it. If the wind changed drastically, the tower could rotate this wind "T" to either north or south so incoming planes could tell which way to land. This young man made a three-point landing square on top of this "T." The plane was kind of matted to it. Getting it off took some serious work.

Our new class included twenty West Point seniors, all of whom were highly rated. They had taken and passed their final exams two months early and then gone through the pre-flight test in Santa Ana, California. There they took hundreds of tests designed to weed out the unqualified. Among other grilling and chilling experiences, they were put in pressure tank chambers where high altitudes were simulated. They took their written tests in an iron room bombarded with almost deafening blows from a large steel hammer. At the same time, sirens and other sorts of monstrous noises squealed and squawked until they'd completed the exam.

One Monday morning the West Pointers marched out in a beautiful close-order drill. They were distributed around by fives so they wouldn't all be in one flight. We were lined up as usual according to height, the idea being that tall and short instructors saw things differently. The first five peeled off and halted directly in front of me. This had been prearranged, though I didn't know it at the time. They were all good men: Stangle, Conway, Northrup, Hommel, and Orr.

Bobby Orr was tragically killed a couple of months after leaving us. He'd been assigned to a fighter squadron in Texas, flying new P-38 Lightnings. He and his commanding officer were up around fifteen thousand feet in close formation, side by side, talking to each other on their radios, when suddenly Orr didn't respond. His commander looked over and saw Orr's head bent over. He knew immediately what had happened—oxygen failure. He banged his wing against Orr's, but that failed to wake him. The P-38 started down in a long dive. The commander followed him, risking his own life by hitting Orr's plane with his wing, but he had to pull out at the last second. Orr's plane went straight into the Texas desert. They recalled most of that group of P-38s and found oxygen failure in several.

Stangle and Conway both lost their lives in separate planes

*Tom and Elva
in 1946*

*Tom was a passenger in an "Arrow F" when it pan-caked onto a pile of rocks
at the south end of his own air strip at Old Ferry Road. Other than wiping out
the radiator, there was little serious damage. This plane was called "The
brother to the brick." Tom agreed: "Without full throttle this plane knew only
one direction—down."*

1940. Tom and the WACO UPF-7 he used to teach the aerobatic portion of
the CPT (Civil Pilot Training) Program just prior to World War II.

Top: One of the first planes Tom owned was a Aeronca Champion.

Middle: The Waco UPF-7 Tom used to teach the aerobatic portion of the CPT Program just prior to World War II.

Above: According to Tom, the Fairchild 24-G (the plane he used to fly two insurance men from Medford to Coos Bay in a bad storm) was a good, dependable plane.

Top: The Beech D-17 was the top of the line, according to Tom. "It could pull right up beside United's DC-3 and pass."

Right: Tom preparing to give flight instructions to a student.

flying B-17s on a night raid over Germany the night before Christmas.

About this time, the so-called experts decided on a way that we could speed things up to get out more pilots faster. As it was, the cadets took pre-flight exams, went on to Primary, where they flew Stearmans, and then to Basic to fly the Vultee BT-13, a plane equipped with radio and instruments for instrument flying. These experts had the idea that they could save money by skipping the Primary stage and going right to using the BT-13s. The new orders were for each Flight to familiarize their instructors in the new plane. A Flight was chosen first, and Frank Ralston, senior commander of A and B Flights, was checked out at the nearest basic training center. He brought one of the BT-13s back with him, and I was chosen to fly it and to check out the A Flight.

The BT-13 was much easier to fly than a Stearman, as well as being better in aerobatics. It had a 450–horsepower engine, a tremendous help, but with the radio and instruments it was hardly a trainer for primary work. Learning on this plane would not qualify the students to fly the more advanced AT-6 with its narrow retractable landing gear and a 650–horsepower engine if they were to go into fighters. Furthermore, if they were to fly multi-engine bombers, they'd be going on to multi-engine school. Not only that, but the BT-13s were very expensive planes, and a ground loop could cost the price of three or four Stearmans. I had no choice, though, but to go ahead and check out the instructors. Then I waited. Three weeks later they came and took the BT-13 away. That was the last we ever heard of that, thank goodness.

However, while the plane was still at Rankin, Frank and I went up on a routine flight. I was eager to show off how well the BT-13 did aerobatics, so I dove down to get speed up for an Immelman— a half-loop with a roll out to level flight on top of the loop. Just as I reached an airspeed of a hundred and seventy miles per hour, there was a tremendous thump that shook the whole plane, and the plexiglass windshield was suddenly blotted red. When we got squared around, we found that the entire radio antenna mast, made of heavy aluminum-alloy casting, was gone. We'd hit a buzzard, though we didn't know it until we'd landed. The black feathers pasted on the plane and the wicked odor were the give-aways. He had hit the bottom of our propeller and been slung up against the windshield and into the antenna mast.

Army stupidity was not unusual. One example was the requirement that when the allotted time was up, the cadets had to go to basic even if they had just half of their sixty hours in. The winter fog made it difficult to drive to the field, and it made flying dangerous. On one of those foggy days, Howie called to tell me to go outside and listen. It was still foggy, and though I couldn't see a plane, I could hear an engine diving and pulling up, diving and pulling up. It was definitely the sound of a plane in trouble in instrument conditions. I heard the sound of a diving spiral—an unmistakable sound, lower and lower—then the horrendous thud when the plane hit. I jumped in my car and drove in the direction the sound had come from. Near the edge of town I followed a crowd of people running to the Beechcraft Staggerwing that had hit nose-down in a small vacant lot. Two Navy officers and a sailor were dead inside. None were wearing parachutes, though there were five in the baggage compartment. Another case of a non-instrument pilot trying to fly on instruments.

Since Rankin was rated number one of all the Primary Flight Schools, the bureaucrats were curious to find out what made us the best. They visited and arranged to question the instructors. Once we were assembled, they asked what our hobbies were. This provoked much laughter since one of the favorite hobbies was to see how much beer one could hold. When they got to the questions about education, there were only two of us who raised our hands when asked if any had not completed the eighth grade—the oldest instructor there (a real pro) and I.

A couple of weeks later one of the men returned and asked to see me. He'd checked my records, saw that I was an Assistant Flight Commander, and said he'd like to test me. That was okay by me. It took the better part of the afternoon, most of it involving reading and comprehension. I was an avid reader, so I had no problem with that, but I was weak on math. When the exam was completed, he offered me a highschool equivalency in case I ever needed to prove my intelligence. I declined. It seemed to me it would be like sneaking in the back door when I wasn't welcome at the front.

Near the end of the war Rankin Academy had a surprise visitor—a Rankin graduate, Major Richard Bong, the leading ace of the Pacific Theater, with forty confirmed victories. All three hundred and twenty cadets and eighty instructors gathered in front of the main two-story building. Major Bong walked out and stood on the edge of the flat roof. There was dead silence. He put his hands in his pants pockets, looked out at us, and said simply, "Hi guys." The roar of the cadets was so loud that I'm sure it was heard a mile away. The simple act of putting his hands in his pockets—something just not done by an officer said to the cadets, "I'm one of you." He didn't give a speech, but just talked to those young men standing before him as if he were one of them. Major Bong had just returned to the States and was on his way home to Poplar, Wisconsin to marry his girlfriend. A few months later, through no fault of his own, he was killed test-flying the first jet fighter. It was a flame out—an engine problem just after take off.

The war had been going on for two years. Rankin had graduated thousands of cadets, without a single collision in the air, except for the two young pilots who violated the rule of five hundred feet between planes in the air. The only exception to that rule was the early morning take-off when half the planes left the pattern and flew to the auxiliary field. On their return, they'd come in trailing each other in the pattern. As they made the final turn to land alternately, one would land in the left lane and the other in the right lane. It had worked perfectly for two years.

The fifteen- to twenty-mile area they used was a flight area governed by the Air Corps. Suddenly, the CAA barged in to shut them down because they had too many planes too close together in the flight pattern. I was called to Tex Rankin's office and asked to fly one of the officials around, entering and coming in right in the middle of the evening return. We re-entered just as the planes were thickest. They were about two hundred feet apart, nose to tail. As I followed the plane ahead, the official was hollering, "Five hundred feet! Five hundred feet!" at me, pointing to the plane ahead. When we made the final turn toward the field, the plane ahead took the right lane and I took the left. We both landed and taxied quickly to get off onto the taxiway.

"You were too close to the plane ahead," the official scolded me. "You could have rammed it from behind, and the plane in back of us could have easily rammed us."

"Have you ever flown a Stearman?" I asked him.

"No," he said.

"Well, if I had opened the throttle, how long do you think it would have taken us to catch up to the plane ahead?" I asked.

"Just a few seconds," he said.

The Stearman is an excellent trainer, but it isn't built for speed, and has very slow acceleration. At regular cruising speed it would take several miles, not feet, for another Stearman to catch up to or pass it, and that's why we could have such good, tight patterns. Once Rankin explained this, we never heard another word, but why they should have questioned us with our record of safety didn't make any sense in the first place.

We did have a couple of catastrophes, but they were caused by acts of nature. The wind came out of nowhere early one morning and within five minutes was up to gale force. Our men were flying off the east side of the main building. The wind was so strong that Howie and I watched as the roof of one of the cadets' barracks lifted off in one huge piece and sailed like a disc across the parade ground and crashed. It was close to the end of the hour and the planes were coming in to land. Most of the cadets saw they couldn't handle it and flew to auxiliary fields. Those who tried to land in that cross-wind were flipped over on their backs or blown backwards into another plane. The wind had blown many planes onto a pile beside our ready room. One plane still had its engine running on idle with its propeller cutting chunks out of the plane under it. I was afraid it would start a fire and burn them all, so I ran over and began climbing up the pile. When I'd gotten about ten feet up, the entire pile started to lift up. I decided I'd rather be a live coward than a dead hero. I got out of there.

Twenty minutes later the wind was gentle again and the rest of the planes circled and came in to land. We'd lost thirty or forty planes, but no lives. After a check was made, we found only one plane and cadet were missing. We searched the area, but no sign of him. Just before dark the tower got a phone call from a farmer outside the area, to the east. Our pilot had done as he'd been told: Stay with the plane until help comes. He'd asked the farmer to call us. He had landed directly downwind, and with a landing speed of fifty miles per hour and the wind blowing at eighty miles per hour, he'd hit the ground at a hundred and thirty miles per hour. The track across the field showed at least a mile-long run before it ended going up a steep hill. He was alternately praised and called dumb, but he had survived probably the fastest Stearman landing ever made. This cadet had only a few hours of solo, yet he had landed the plane safely in a field without a scratch.

It was the deadly fog that claimed one of our cadets. The winter morning began without a cloud in the sky. Several planes had already taken off, and Hank and I were walking out to get in our planes when, out of the blue, a Stearman came down in a dive and pulled up just in time to keep from crashing. He was going crossways to the runway. Seconds later another plane came down in a spin, hitting nose-first in a horrendous crash. As we were running over to the crashed plane, we heard another plane in a dive. By then the entire end of the field was in a heavy fog. I dropped my chute and ran for the tower. I threw a rock at the tower to get his attention, but when that failed I rushed up the stairs and grabbed the light out of his hands. Too out of breath to talk, all I could do was point to that wall of fog. He wasn't to blame, since he was facing the other end of the field. The man who should have been watching that end of the field was having his breakfast. He'd figured it was safe for him to leave since the weather was so clear.

I'd seen this sort of thing happen before in Medford when the United planes would come in streaming a white cloud behind them. It looked like they were towing a huge white sheet. When the temperature and the dew point are close together, a plane passing through will cool the air just enough for it to condense into fog. That's exactly what happened at Rankin. The first few planes got through, but the rest cooled the air into a blanket of fog. The cadet was still alive by the time I got back to him, but he died four hours later.

We had a good instructor at Rankin who had a habit of staying up half the night and showing up the next day half-asleep. One morning he took his first cadet up to demonstrate a spin and recovery. In a regular spin, the throttle is closed and the nose brought up into a climbing altitude until the plane runs out of airspeed. The stick is then held all the way back tight, with full rudder held to one side or the other. In a regular recovery, the stick is returned to the neutral position and the rudder released, which leaves the plane in a steep dive but easily brought up to level flight. In a Stearman, the recovery is different. The recovery is demonstrated using more force than necessary, but it always stops the spin at once. The pilot bangs the stick all the way past neutral to the stop, centers the rudder, and then brings the stick back to neutral. The only trouble with this is that a second of leaving the stick in the full forward position sends the plane down to an almost vertical dive for a second and the occupants get thrown up against their seat belts. Well, this half-awake instructor demonstrated the spin recovery and told the cadet to try it. Then he waited, and waited, and waited some more. He yelled, "Spin it!" Still nothing happened. When he finally turned around to see why nothing was happening, there was no cadet. He'd fallen out. The instructor searched the area, then returned to the field in a panic, yelling that we should get a search going for his cadet. With that, he took off again to resume his own search.

The truth is that the cadet was safely in the ready room when the instructor first called for the search. We were letting him continue the search to teach him a lesson. When the cadet had fallen out, he'd had the good sense to pull his rip cord and float down. He'd made a good, soft landing in a pasture a couple of miles from Rankin, and the farmer had returned him to us. Both were to blame really—the cadet for not having his safety belt on and the instructor for not checking to see that he had it on.

One accident was especially painful for me. Eugene Crites, a good student of mine in my CPT class in Medford, had joined the Army Air Corps as a cadet and gotten his Primary at another school. He'd gone to basic training at an Army field west of Bakersfield. His instructor took Crites and two other cadets on a routine cross-country flight to a field near Palmdale and they were to return that same day. Crites and another cadet were to fly solo while the instructor had the third man fly with him. When he got to Palmdale, he was told that fog was rolling in and he'd have to hold off returning until the next day. It was Saturday and the instructor had a date that night. He didn't listen. He ordered Crites and the other cadet to fly formation on his plane and he'd fly on instruments leading them home. Unfortunately, the instructor wasn't sharp on the gauges. He kept getting lower and lower, and suddenly he saw water right under his wheels. He made a sharp pull up, but when he leveled off, he and his passenger were alone. When he arrived in Bakersfield, he couldn't even tell anyone where he'd been over the water, he'd been so far off the course. The following spring a seat cushion was found in Castaic Lake. The serial number on it was from Crite's plane. Both planes were found about a year after that when the lake was very low.

Because of a gall bladder problem, Tex Rankin had been unable to fly for sometime. He had recovered and had been secretly flying in preparation for a surprise aerobatic show for the cadets. When the day came, the cadets were gathered on the balcony and the roof of the Army quarters. Tex did his entire act within a hundred feet of the spectators. He took off in his little Ryan at the far end of the field and disappeared from view. His plane was a low-winged monoplane with a Menasco engine he'd won his world championship in. Suddenly, here he came doing an inverted square loop trailing a coil of dense red smoke about two feet in diameter, lasting about ten seconds. He dove down directly vertical to the ground for several hundred feet, then made an almost square to inverted turn and shot along with his helmet not three feet off the ground. He followed that with another square turn. Then he shot straight up and made another inverted turn until he hit the other end of the first smoke, leaving an almost perfect square of red smoke.

He shut off the system with the red smoke as he got to the end of the first maneuver. Next, he flew up and turned back to do a double snap roll around the red smoke with blue smoke. This made it look like the blue smoke was knotted over the red. A beautiful circle of blue smoke appeared with the knot of red just before he did triple snap rolls right down until the smoke was bouncing off the runway. Then, he did tail slides, letting the plane slide down backwards and flatten out within three or four feet of the ground.

After that he treated us to the maneuver he'd won many contests with—one that no one else dared do right down off the deck at the finish. It was an inverted thirteen-turn spin. He turned it so perfectly that on the last turn the smoke bounced on the ground. His head looked like it was only about three feet above the pavement again. He performed for twenty minutes without a break before leaving in a long, continuous, slow roll in an absolute straight line away from us. A long corkscrew of smoke followed for about a mile. The cadets cheered themselves hoarse. It was a sight to behold.

Surely, that was what we remembered when we heard about Rankin's fatal plane crash. A couple of years after the war he'd gotten a distributorship for a new design of a four- to five-place amphibian airplane. He was flying it out of Klamath Falls, a good field except for power lines on the north end. On this particular summer afternoon he was offering free rides. It was his last flight of the day, and he had four passengers with him. When he got to the power lines, he found he was a little too short of clearing them. Rather than diving under, he tried to go over, but the wheels caught the wires and the plane went down. No one survived to tell the story. What perplexed us was that Rankin always stressed in his lectures that in an emergency situation like that pilots were always to go under, never over. Rankin's son also lost his life flying. He was shot down by anti-aircraft fire in Europe.

It was 1945, the end of the war was in sight, and we'd received word that since there would only be a few cadets in the next class, a couple of the Flights would be eliminated. I'd kept in touch with Silas throughout my time at Rankin, so I knew his business had been reduced to nothing but repairs and that there were no new planes of any kind. Always one to look for new opportunities, it didn't take Silas long to find one. Did I want to join him?

Chapter 13

The Francie

Silas had spent seven years on steamships and knew the ocean well. I, on the other hand, had never been on a steamship, but I loved to fish, and that's what my friend had in mind. Commercial fishing had suffered because of imposed regulations during the war, but now with the end of the war approaching, there were lots of good fishing boats for sale and the price of fish was rising. We'd be going after Chinook salmon and tuna. I said my goodbyes to Rankin, and Elva and I headed for Oregon. (It was on that trip we heard on our car radio that President Roosevelt had died.)

Silas and I found the Francie W. in a mooring basin by the Columbia River. She was a converted sailing hull with a Chrysler engine. We agreed that I'd take care of the fishing, and since he was a registered ship's pilot, he'd run the boat. After we figured out what we'd need to outfit the boat, we said a sad but excited farewell to our wives and sailed down the river to Astoria. That's where the large fish canneries were, most of which had been started about a hundred years before by a community of Finns.

No matter how prepared we told ourselves we were, we knew that navigating through the Columbia Bar would be the most dangerous part of our trip. It had claimed the lives of many men and ships each year. The bar was six miles long and unpredictable. We decided our safest way would be to situate our boat right in the middle of a flock of boats and cross the bar with them. Once we were safely out, we watched to see when they threw their lines out and then we followed suit. Just as I let the last line out, I noticed one of the poles shaking. I pulled in four large salmon. After that the fish came so fast and furiously that before I could get all of the fish off all of the lines, we'd already have more fish on the first ones. Then just as quickly as they'd come, they were gone. We cruised around, following the other boats until another school was found. We kept a close watch on those boats all day, and when they started back across the bar, we tagged right along with them again.

It wasn't until we got close to Astoria that we discovered a serious mistake we'd made. All of those wonderful salmon we'd caught had to be cleaned and gutted, and it should have been done in the v-shaped trough in the trolling pit as we pulled them aboard. It was almost dark by the time we pulled into the cove. We were mighty thankful for the gas engine Silas had rigged up to power our little generator with its feeble light bulb. We needed that light to clean over two hundred salmon. It took us until almost daylight. We had learned our lesson the hard way.

We got pretty good after that. There would be days when we'd have thirty-two separate lures in the water with a fish on every hook at the same time. It was on a day when the bar was deemed impassable that we met Glen Brooks. Glen had a reputation for fishing no matter how bad the storms were. That day we watched his boat, the Aleutian, battle her way across the bar and slip into a dock near us. He was intrigued with the way I had rigged up a motor with a buffing wheel to polish our lures, which tended to get dull after a week or two in the water. Since the lures attracted the fish, it was important to keep them shiny, but most fisherman simply threw them away and put new ones on. We couldn't afford to do that.

Glen invited us to go down to Newport, his home port, to run partner boat with him fishing for tuna. We accepted and agreed to meet him there. We had enough confidence by then that we left on a day the Coast Guard warned that the bar was rough, but passable. A Navy ship, the cruiser Salt Lake, was going out just ahead of us. Suddenly, the waves were the biggest I'd ever seen them. One minute the bow of the Salt Lake pointed up about forty degrees, the next minute it would be nose down with the pilot house window completely under water. That ship was being tossed all over the place, and anything not tied down was sliding from one side to the other. As we passed her, it looked like a hundred sailors hanging onto the railing tossing their lunches into the river. The Salt Lake had just come from Swan Island Shipyard where she'd been refitted. Now she had to turn around and go right back to be refitted again.

We'd lost everything on our own deck, but we got out to sea, and we knew then that we had bought ourselves a good, seaworthy boat. Our arrangement with Glen turned out to be a good idea. Most tuna boats run in pairs, since they go out in blue water over two hundred miles off shore. A wreck or engine failure could leave a single boat in big trouble. Small boats like ours would be out of sight over the horizon in eight miles. We had a successful and profitable season with Glen.

I must admit we did chance it alone once, and it was a foolish thing to do. We got off to a bad start and it didn't get any better. No sooner did we reach blue water, when we felt a big bump. Our engine shook wildly. Silas shut it off immediately. I peeled off my clothes and dove under the stern to look at the propeller. Three blades had broken off, which had caused the tremendous imbalance that was being transferred down the shaft to the engine. We were about two hundred miles west of land, and though Silas was an excellent mechanic, he hadn't the foggiest idea how to fix the propeller. He tried running the engine very slowly and found that at about a quarter throttle, the vibration was still there, but the boat didn't shake as much as it had. The Francie moved along about three miles an hour, then, after thirty minutes, the engine would overheat and we'd have to turn it off. Fortunately we had a steady sail, a triangular sail fixed behind the mast and hauled up tight as possible to keep the boat from rolling from side to side. We experimented with the sail and found that by hauling it out at a right angle it would give us more speed.

With only a radio receiver, we had to navigate by compass and the sun. Our deepest fear was that we'd be hit by a storm. Sure enough, that came too. The clouds rolled in and the winds quickly reached gale force. The seas got higher, making it harder and harder to steer. At first we took turns at the wheel, an hour at a time. Eventually the wheel kicked so hard it would lift me right off the deck. I could stand at the wheel for only twenty minutes, then ten, and finally I lasted only five. We were both exhausted, but we couldn't give in. If we turned sideways, we'd roll over and be done for.

After what seemed more like a week than a night, daylight came, and we could tell by the volume on the radio that we were getting closer to home. The storm center had passed, but the seas were worse than ever. When we looked behind us, the enormous deep sea rollers looked taller than our mast. We nursed that old Chrysler engine with all our wit and might until at last we saw land. We limped into dock at Astoria going two miles an hour. We fell into our beds and slept twelve straight hours.

Two days later, with a new propeller and valves and an overhauled engine, the Francie was ready to go again. I'll never forget the night I replaced Silas at the wheel. It was a very dark night and much warmer than usual. The sea was wonderful with long, easy rollers, and then suddenly, every displaced drop of water off the curl of a wave, particularly in the wake behind our propeller, shone like phosphorus. The curl of those waves made long, sparkling streams. This was my first introduction to foxfire, and it lasted for a couple of hours. That night was the first time I really felt at home out there on the ocean.

And I'll surely never forget the very next day returning to the dock and being met by cheers and hurrahs and my wife running up crying, "The war is over!" Elva and I sat up late that night talking about the bomb America had dropped on Japan.

With the war over, Silas and I decided it was time to sell the Francie and return home. We hoped it would only take a couple of weeks to sell her. It took a day. The Francie went off to fish in Alaska, and Elva and I went home to Shady Cove. I was so happy to be back home, and more than pleased that Elva liked Shady Cove as much as I did. I started silversmithing again, and whenever we could, Elva and I would go fishing and hunting together.

Elva has another version of this: It's true, we did do some fishing and hunting together. I thoroughly enjoyed fishing, until the time I caught such a big fish that I was sure it would pull me right into the water. It scared me to death. I never went again after that. That happened right here in front of our house on the river. And, yes, before the boys came along, we'd go hunting together. I remember once when I was dogging for him, I was eating chocolate and having a great time, even in the rain, when all of a sudden I heard a shot. I fell to the ground, frightened out of my wits. When I finally got brave enough to get up, I found Tom with the deer. I just wanted to cry.

One time when we were out hunting, and it got toward evening, we decided to spend the night out. We settled down by a big log and Tom went right to sleep. My gosh, he slept right through, but my teeth were chattering so hard, I was afraid to close my mouth for fear the racket would wake him up. He thought it was great. I thought it was a terrible night. I never did that again either.

My dad and Tom put a dummy deer up once as a practical joke on friends of ours who weren't very good hunters. From a distance that deer looked real. They even put shiny aluminum eyes on him. Our friends fell for it, shot it again and again, and when it didn't fall over, they even crept up and poked it with their rifle butt.

As for Whittaker, he and the other pre-war dealers and manufacturers were sure the boom times were just around the corner. Certainly, they thought, all those pilots who had learned to fly in the war would want their own planes. Apparently they didn't. To make matters worse, the government sold the training planes at junk prices. Stearmans went for as low as five dollars apiece in lots of a hundred. BT-13s went for less than two hundred dollars—their large, 450-horsepower P&W engines cost ten times that much new. Thousands of planes were scrapped. No one would even look at a 65–horsepower Cub. (Whittaker had sold my 60–horsepower Cub Sport after I left his place in 1941.) He found himself a job as a parts man for a new outfit selling Aeronca and Stinson airplanes. Eventually he was able to get me a new Aeronca 65–horsepower Champ.

Before I knew it, I was back in airplanes. Hugh, one of my former CPT students, asked if I'd instruct him so he could get his rating. He had his commercial license, but not his instructor's rating. The CAA had caught him instructing for a man named Ernie, who had a small airport west of Medford. Ernie was a Taylor Craft dealer and had just begun operating this new field. He had only three or four pre-war Taylor Crafts, a two-place monoplane, an old Fairchild four-place cabin plane, and an old Beechcraft Biplane —a three- or four-place cabin plane with a 220-horsepower engine. I agreed to instruct Hugh and also instruct for Ernie. Ernie was struggling—he and his wife were living in a metal hangar that sat out in the open without shade of any kind. It had to be a hot, miserable place to live.

The Taylor Craft was a fine small plane, but it had one dangerous feature: the engine was set up too high, which in a slight climb made it hard to see out the front. There had been several fatalities already because of this, so I always stressed the importance of climbing in a slight turn, especially if they were flying into the sun. I had a friend who had a couple of Taylor Crafts and was teaching at a field near Ashland. The day I went over to see him, both planes were out when I got there, but only one plane came back in. It was my friend and his student, both badly shaken. They'd collided with his other plane that was being flown solo by a student pilot. About a foot of my friend's plane had been torn off at the end of the right wing. "We were flying straight and level when it happened," he told me. "We were both looking at something on the ground, when a strong jolt spun us halfway around. By the time we got squared up again, we couldn't see the other plane."

He took off again to search for the other plane, but after twenty minutes he returned, no sign of the plane. Just about then we heard a plane flying very slowly toward the field. The pilot made a fairly good landing, despite the fact that he had a good bit missing from his left wing and a great deal of fabric hanging loose. Another example of the Taylor Craft's weakness.

One afternoon Ernie asked me to fly a couple of men to Cave Junction, about forty miles west. The Fairchild was already gassed up and ready to go when I got there. Since there were no gas tanks at the field, gas was brought in and pumped from fifty-gallon drums. I decided to go over the mountains, as it was shorter than following the valley. I climbed higher and higher and then, just past the halfway point and as I was starting my descent, the engine suddenly popped and sputtered for a second or two and then sounded normal again. Had it quit then, I would have had no possible landing site, so I turned off toward farmland. It happened several more times, and each time I picked a field and approached it, but each time the engine came back on. By the time we limped into Cave Junction, I could barely keep the plane up. I jumped out to check the tank. It was full of a mixture of rusty, dirty gas and water. I knew exactly what had happened, and it didn't make me very happy. Ernie had topped off the tanks in the Fairchild with gas from a couple of old gas barrels about a quarter full that no one used anymore. I called Ernie and told him we'd be spending the night. In the mornings, we carefully drained out all of the gas. Since water is heavier than gas, it sank to the bottom of the fuel tank. I had the operator take photographs of over three quarts of that filthy water we took out of the tank.

If I'd had any doubts about the source of the problem, they were gone when I landed at Ernie's field the next day. There were two holes in the ground where the rusty barrels had been sitting. "I admit I moved those barrels, but I certainly have no idea how the dirty gas and water got into the Fairchild," Ernie was quick to tell me. Nevertheless, he paid for our night's lodging and the new gas. You can be sure I never set foot on that field again.

That ended my flying for a spell. I went back to silversmithing, though I also spent a good bit of time fixing up our place and working some in the local logging industry, where many new sawmills were starting up.

Since Elva and I were doing all of our cooking and heating with firewood, that meant we had to gather a cord and a half of wood a year. We learned one lesson the hard way. We had used a cross saw (also called a misery whip) to saw off a cylinder about eighteen inches long and thirty inches across from a Douglas fir log we found up in the hills behind our place. We set it on its side and sent it rolling down the hill. It rolled well. Too well! It rolled itself all the way to the river and floated away. We found that rolling the cylinders at an angle worked much better. Actually, the best fuel was chunks of Douglas fir bark, as much as a foot thick and easily broken up into long slabs. That way we could take them home and split them into any size. They burned much like coal, glowing red but with no flame. Once we had the jeep it was easy to go back into the forest and haul it home.

We were expecting our first child in April, and for a number of reasons, Elva wanted to be with her parents in Tulare when the baby was born. She flew to California in early January. She had faith in Dr. Burton. He had taken care of her in 1940 when she'd had polio, so that was one good reason. Another was that our outhouse was at the end of a long path. Another was that any time she wanted water, she had to go out on the back porch where our pitcher pump was. Also, we had no phone, our jeep was our only means of transportation, and we were twenty miles from Medford. Who could blame her?

While she was away, I used the time to make things a little easier for her on her return. I changed the hand pump to a pressure pump, completed the bathroom, and got water to the kitchen sink. Because of the continuous rain, I couldn't fly my Aeronca to Tulare until April 19. It was excellent timing—Arthur Ross Tepper was born at three o'clock the next morning. Unfortunately, Elva developed strep throat and she and the baby weren't able to return to Shady Cove until early June.

During that time I was asked to teach a class at a lapidary club in Grants Pass. The members were rock hounds who found, cut, and polished agates and other semi-precious stones, but none of them knew how to make settings for the stones. The class was limited to a dozen students. The best of them was an eighty-year-old woman who was also the local pharmacologist.

Chapter 14

AG Flying

The next spring I had a visit from Tom Bowles, a friend and fellow Rankin instructor, who came to ask if I'd help out. He had moved to a small city near Yuba, California where he had a fast-growing agricultural flying service. He had six Travelair Biplanes and not enough pilots to fly them during the peak season, April until mid June. Of course I said yes. That meant flying again. I wasn't about to say no.

The Travelair Biplanes had been fitted for ag work with a single seat for the pilot. An area ahead of the pilot had been converted into a hopper to hold twenty hundred-pound sacks of fertilizer or seed. These planes were originally powered with the 90–horsepower OX5 engines, but these planes had 300–horsepower Lycoming engines with constant speed propellers. The extra horsepower gave them spectacular performance and made them very maneuverable, essential for this type of flying. I'd flown Travelairs before, but none with this engine.

Each of us had our own plane. No matter how closely a plane is made to the same specifications, each plane flies a little differently. They all had good air speed indicators, and all of us ag pilots were to hold as close as possible to ninety miles per hour when we released the seed or fertilizer.

First, our hoppers had to be loaded. If a pilot, for example, had a 640–acre field to seed that needed a hundred pounds of fertilizer per acre, he needed a truck to deliver six 100-pound sacks, plus one forty-pound sack to a landing strip near the field. A loader with an eight-foot chute dumped the fertilizer into the hopper. The pilot then flew to the field, where a couple of flaggers were each holding a tall bamboo fishing rod with a white flag, each flagger about eight feet from the end of opposite sides of the field. The pilot's job was to fly right over the first flagger at about ten feet, and to pull a lever to release the material, all the while aiming for the other flagger and flying right over his head as he pulled the lever shut. He then pulled up, made a turn and went back. While the pilot was turning, the flaggers took eight paces more so that the pilot would cover a twenty-four-foot swath on each pass. At ninety miles per hour, he was moving at a hundred and thirty-two feet per second, which meant in order to start and stop the flow from the hopper, he had to operate the gate in mini-seconds.

The ag planes had no windshields, which meant our heads and necks were out in ninety miles per hour winds all day. For the first few days of each season, my neck got so tired from the pressure, I could hardly sleep. Goggles and helmets were a necessity, as were the rags to wipe the oil and bugs off our goggles. Sore and cracked lips went along with the job.

The only instruments we had to watch were the oil pressure, air speed, and the tachometer for the engine RPM. We each had a loader, who kept track of the time to refuel the plane every hour. But we had to be alert every single moment, as there were dozens of hazards to be aware of. Power lines were responsible for most of the fatal accidents, though flights of wild ducks and trees took their share of lives. Every field and every day was different. For example, the air was cool when we left at gray daylight, about an hour before sun-up, so we could carry more wieght. By noon, when the air was warmer, we'd have to carry three or four fewer sacks, otherwise we couldn't take off from the short strips. By late afternoon, we could add a sack or two again. Any wind would foul up the air speed. Adjustments had to be made automatically—there was no time to stop and figure out what to do next.

We had no gauges to regulate the flow of the seed, thus we regulated it according to each situation. And there was no acceptable excuse for running short of rice seed. If seed was left over, we could always fly back and scatter a little more, but if we were short, there was no way for the farmer to run quickly and stratify more seed to plant.

Many farmers built swimming pools and wrote them off on their taxes, saying they used their pools to soak their seed. Some actually did too. Others soaked their bags of seeds in the dirty water in the ditches, where the seeds accumulated clay and silt, making them slick as glass. These seeds went out of the sacks much quicker. All this had to be factored in when we determined how much to let out at a time. Also for tax purposes, farmers often claimed their fields were smaller than they actually were making it that much more difficult to gauge the amount of seed.

Being a perfectionist didn't make the job an easy one for me. I really sweated over it at first. There were so many details to keep track of. It took awhile before I was used to looking back over my shoulder to see if my swath was smooth and symmetrical. If something had gotten caught in the spreader where the material passed through, it could leave a blank space that would show up later in the crops.

Tom Bowles and his brother John each weighed two hundred and fifty pounds. I weighed less than a hundred and fifty. That meant I could haul one more hundred-pound sack, which meant by the end of the day I would usually be fifty sacks ahead of them. I often flew with John that first year. He was a tremendous help in teaching me how to set and fine-tune the hopper gate.

Each season began with fertilizing the fields. I was flying in the Sacramento Valley, where rice was the major crop. The rice fields were sectioned off in irregular, separate fields with dikes, and were flooded with about a foot of water. It looked like we were flying over lakes. After the rice had been soaking in burlap bags under water for three to five days, depending on the variety, it would begin to sprout. At that point it had to be sown, otherwise the sprouts would get so long they'd tangle and break off. If it was sown dry, it would float into solid patches on top of the water and leave too many bare spots. This was the most critical time of the season and we flew from "can't see to can't see," putting in up to sixteen hours a day, including debriefing and planning. This meant I was buying my food in town, cooking a late supper in a motel, cooking my own breakfast in the morning, and heating a can of soup for my thermos for lunch. I sure missed Elva's good cooking.

There was one field that I particularly dreaded flying over. It had power lines just past the end, and though John had shown me how to go under them rather than over, it took awhile before I got over my apprehension.

The season lasted for six long weeks. I was so beat at the end that I took a day to rest before going home to Shady Cove. I spent that winter much like I had the year before: working on our house, enjoying my new son, teaching, and silver working.

The next spring when I returned to Live Oak, I found a surprise waiting for me. My Travelair 4421 now had brand new wings made by an old wing maker in Marysville. They greatly improved the plane's performance. I also got to hire my own loader and crew that year. I chose Garcia, a local resident, for my loader, and several other Hispanics for my crew. They were good, hard workers. Most were here illegally who crossed the border to spend the spring and summer working, then returned to Mexico for the winter. At the end of each afternoon they'd call out, "Una mas" (one more) after each loading. Many other loaders would complain and beg to quit early if the weather was cold and rainy, but never these men. With this crew I could get out about five extra loads a day, seventy-five hundred pounds more than before.

Bowles lost two good Travelairs that season because one of his new pilots hadn't paid attention while he was filling his gas tank. To refuel, the pilot leaves the engine running while he gets out and removes the gas cap in the center section of the upper wing. Someone else passes him the hose, he carefully puts the nozzle in the tank, and waves to signify the okay to pump. This careless pilot had his mind elsewhere. When the gas hit the engine, there was a huge ball of fire and in an instant the plane was burning. A plane parked right off his wing caught fire, and in less than two minutes both planes were gone.

Ag flying was considered so dangerous that only one other group of workers was rated as a higher risk by insurance companies —the men who dug the tunnels under rivers in caissons (structures with compressed air to keep the water out). For every dollar Bowles paid his pilots, he paid sixty cents to the insurance company.

When I went back to Shady Cove at the end of that season in June, I did some carpentry work, something I'd never done much of before. I still wasn't much good at math, but with Elva's help and the aid of books we managed to tear down Bristow's small cabin and use that wood to build a shop. I put a lean-to shed roof on one end and set up a blacksmith shop in it. I could now forge out bridle bits again.

More important, that fall we had another addition to our family. John was born September 25, 1950. Elva was busier than ever now, and I resumed teaching the jewelry making class in Grants Pass one night a week. That year one of my most talented students was a butcher. He created a handmade carousel using twenty-two pounds of sterling silver and hundreds of different semi-precious cabochons. (All gems or semi-gems are cut and polished in one of two styles: Precious gems like diamonds, emeralds, and rubies were facet-cut with many facets or small flats. Other gems cut and polished in cabochon—without facets—and they're called cabs.) That butcher is long gone, but the carousel is still being shown in rock exhibits all over the country. Also I bought some lapidary equipment and began producing stones to sell, mostly local agates and petrified wood that made simple but eye-catching things.

Before I knew it, it was April and time to go back to Live Oak. This time they gave me some of the large acreages to work, plus some new farms. But it was another farm that gave me cause for constant alarm that year. There was a dam with an electric generating plant below it on the Sacramento River above Redding. The main electric cables from the plant went down to Sacramento on towers up to a hundred feet high, stretching across the land like one long fence, with farmlands under some of them. My new farm had a great deal of rice land on each side as well as under the power lines. Because there wasn't enough room to fly safely underneath, I had to fly up close to the wires on the tower, haul up and over, and then dive down the other side. Each time I'd pull up to go over the tip, I was aware just how dangerous those seconds were. Then one morning I found I was getting a little more oil on my goggles than usual. Just as I pulled over the top of the wires and let down on the other side, my goggles were suddenly completely coated. That meant I had a bad leak and I'd better head back to base. One of the nine large cylinders had a vertical crack from top to bottom, wide enough to push a knife blade through. "Tommy, you not only had the rabbit's foot with you, you had the whole rabbit," John Bowles said.

Ritchie, the mechanic, rolled the plane into the hangar, pulled out the engine and went to work. Normally, it took two people working for twenty-four hours to take off the engine and propeller and replace them. When I checked the next morning, my plane was all set to go, and there was Ritchie sound asleep on a cot in the back of the hangar. Ritchie had spent the war as a tailgunner in B17s. The last I heard, he and his wife were sailing across the Pacific to Tahiti. They were in radio contact each day and were fairly close to Tahiti when an early typhoon closed in on them. No one knows what happened to them.

Tom Bowle's had a ranch of his own planted in rice and corn. It was plowed, harrowed and ready to plant when he asked me to fly his fields that year. After I finished, he asked how I'd come out. "Long," I told him, "both for the rice and corn," which meant I had some left over.

"Both John and I always come out long, too," he said, "and that can only mean one of two things: either we're all three wrong, or I don't have the full acreage I'm supposed to have." He had a survey done and found that his neighbor had moved his fence down several hundred feet some years before. That same day, Bowles took a 'cat' and bulldozed the fence down right up to the surveyor's stakes and left it in a big, messy roll.

The following season Bowles presented an offer to me that required a difficult decision. He wanted me to fly for him all year round as his chief pilot. He offered us a beautiful two-story brick house surrounded by old shade trees and flower beds on fourteen acres of deeded ground. "If you agree to come," Bowles promised, "I'll buy it for you and you can live in it as long as you like, or, if you prefer, I can deed it over to you."

I turned it down because of my boys. I just couldn't think of raising them anywhere but here in Shady Cove. We had plenty of room, we were protected on the north and east by government land, and the beautiful Rogue River was our boundary on the west side. What more could we want? I've never regretted that decision.

On November 17, 1951 our son Tim was born. We now had three sons. I spent another season ag flying, and when it was over that June 1952, I helped my friend Raddy Gardener build an irrigation dam on his land. When that was completed, Elva and I designed and built a swimming pool for our boys.

Chapter 15

Tree Seed Business

This could change our lives," I said to Elva one evening in October after reading an article in the paper announcing that the local Bureau of Land Management (BLM) needed pine and fir cones for their reforestation projects. Interested people should contact them, it said. I was definitely interested.

Monday morning I went to their main office in Medford, where John Warnke filled me in on the details. He also told me something that proved very helpful: I could find them where the pine squirrels take the cones and cache them for their winter food. Someone had already found some and brought in several sacks. John Carnegie, another BLM employee there, said he'd heard they were finding them up on Dead Indian Road.

I didn't waste any time. The next morning I took my Ford up to Dead Indian and on past there to the country where I'd spent the summer of 1933. Toward the end of the day, and just when I was ready to give up, I spotted a dead white fir log with a stash of Douglas fir cones in the rotted out end. I found even more on the way back to the car. I filled two sacks full that afternoon, and the BLM paid me well for them. I was in business.

From then on I was better organized. I fitted my jeep, which I could take on the old logging roads, with a tarp so I could cook and sleep under it in bad weather. I now had a much better idea of where to look for the cones. It wasn't a particularly good year for cones, but because I had come to recognize similarities in the caches I found, I had a fairly good first year. It took me a couple more years before I understood why the squirrels cached them where they did. It was to keep them damp. Left out in the open, the sun would dry them, the cones would open, and the seeds would fall out.

I got further into the seed business thanks to a bad fall storm with damaging floods. I had taken my cones to the BLM warehouse near Bear Creek in Medford, laid my twenty sacks out on the concrete floor until they could be sent to a tree-seed extractor near Salem, and I'd gone happily home with the money in my pocket. A couple of days later, after reading that the storm had flooded the BLM warehouse, I rushed over and found my sacks of cones all lumped together in one muddy pile. They'd probably have to be disposed of, I was told. I hated to see them go to waste, so I asked if I could try my hand at salvaging them. I had no idea how to go about it, but I stored them in my woodshed while I thought about it.

I'd often flown over the US Forest Service nursery and seed extractory near Bend. Perhaps I could get some ideas from them. I drove up and met with Charlie Betts, who listened quietly while I presented my problem. The first thing Betts did was to point out all the things I shouldn't do, all the mistakes that had been made in building the extractory. For one, they dried the cones in trays with fine wire mesh bottoms, stacked five feet high in a room that held about fifty stacks. Hot air was blown down through ducts overhead, hitting only the cones in the top screen. So each tray had to be moved every day. Obviously, the air should come up from the bottom. I should also build my extractory on a slope, he said, so the seeds would slide downhill. At Bend, the seeds all had to be carried. I learned more in those four hours than I could have learned in a year somewhere else. Not only that, he shared his lunch with me.

I built a miniature extractory to start with, using a wood stove for heat and a fan to blow the hot air. As Betts suggested, I sent away for a small hand-powered seed cleaner and screens. With this equipment, I could clean ten pounds of seed at a time. I took the first clean seeds to the BLM, and they sent samples to the Oregon State Seed Testing Laboratory to test the germination, purity, and moisture content. Getting the results took a month, but the answer came back positive, and they bought the seed.

Eugene Peterson, the local director of the BLM, asked if I'd be interested in getting tree seed for them on a regular basis since all of the logged-off land had to be replanted. I told him my real love was flying, but since age was going to get me soon anyway, why not? Sure, I'd be interested. John Warnke gave me a book on the general principles of reforestation, and I became a student again.

My future seemed to hold exactly what I'd been looking for: a business of my own in my own place, and one that would give me my time alone. Elva and I immediately began putting up a building that I estimated could store a thousand sacks of cones to start. It was just a roof with racks to keep the cones out of the rain. My son uses that same structure today. After that we started to build a two-story building to dry and open the cones in. We were building it on a hillside so the cones would come in on the upper story. Before this was completed, it was time to go back for what turned out to be my last year of ag flying. When I left the Bowles that year and told them the reason I wouldn't be returning was because I was going into the tree seed business, they called it the "squirrel food business."

My first priority when I got back home was to finish the drying building. We added an annex to hold a device called a tumbler that shakes the seeds out of the cones after they've dried and opened. This was by far the most complicated project we'd done thus far. I bought a new wood-burning furnace and a new seed cleaner with an electric-powered motor. I made screens with wooden sides and ends, and bottoms of wire mesh or hardware cloth. I made cabinets to hold eight screens with metal ducts to carry the hot air up. Now I was ready to start putting out some seeds.

It was to be a good year for ponderosa pine and sugar pine, but no one could know whether the squirrels would cache them. Petersen's men found an area of pine with a good crop of cones near Pinehurst and put out a bid to have it logged that fall, with the provision that the trees be felled one or two at a time so that the cones could be picked. By September, when the cones were ready, we'd hired a few locals, and each day I'd go up to Pinehurst to pay the pickers and haul the cones home in my new GMC pickup.

We soon learned we had competition. The three largest tree-seed dealers in the Northwest were the Manning Tree Seed Company in Washington, the Woods Tree Seed Company in Salem, Oregon, and the Brown Seed Company in Vancouver, Washington. As yet, none of them were collecting in my area, but times were rapidly changing. The BLM and the Forest Service recognized that only brush was coming back up after logging, so, like it or not, they'd have to replant. They had few people who knew how to do this. So many of the different species of trees were found only in my area, so I worried that would bring the outside companies in.

Up until then, little reforestation had been done after the huge virgin old-growth forests had been cut, and in many cases slash, dead branches, and unwanted trees had been set on fire, leaving miles of ashes. In several states, Wisconsin and Minnesota, for example, forest nurseries were beginning to raise seedlings to reforest their treeless acreage. Unfortunately, what they were finding was that the seeds came up but quickly died. They had the same results for several years, and despite chemistry tests, etc., they found no cure. Finally a young man named Hunt was called in. He tracked down a nursery in Corvallis, Oregon where Vern, the owner, had found the answer to the problem, though he hadn't yet discovered the cause. It didn't take Hunt long to find the answer. Vern had fixed his soil simply by bringing in a few buckets of soil from under the forest trees and scattering it on the new soil. Hunt found that tiny little spores called mycorrhizae attach themselves to the roots of the seedling and turn the soil into an element that allows the seedling to get its necessary food from the soil.

Hunt was ecstatic—he now had living proof of a simple cure. He wrote up his notes in detail and mailed them back to the lab in St. Paul before starting home. That night, just past Pendleton, he was pushed off the road into the sagebrush by another car. He was shot to death by a couple of men who took all of his clothes, including the ones he'd been wearing, and his car. The state police found his naked body the next day. A couple of days later, the killers were captured.

As the demand for seed grew, nurseries began popping up all over the Pacific Northwest. I had gotten in just at the beginning of this flourish, so there wasn't much I could copy from the old extractories. I still had dozens of problems to solve and things to learn about the business. I was caught in the arena, though, and if I wanted to stay in business, I had to read and figure things out for myself. For one thing, I needed to familiarize myself with all the trees, their seeds, how they should be handled, and what the process was that caused a seed to form and to produce another living seedling. There was very little in print, and very few people to ask.

It was certainly not a cut-and-dried process. For example, the conifers, trees that bear their seed-bearing fruit in the form of a cone, in my area all have male staminate buds mostly on the lower limbs and the female pistillate buds on the upper limbs. This almost cancels out self-pollination, something nature cannot tolerate since seed produced by self-pollination will generally drop off before ripening, or if it does ripen, the seedlings will be sickly and won't survive. Thus nature has arranged for the wind to blow the lightweight pollen buds away and onto the female flowers in the tops of other trees. This happens in March or April in our area. Warm, windy, kite-flying days are best for pollination.

Then, too, different trees have different size and shaped cones, and different maturation periods. All pines take two years to mature. When their pistillate flowers open, they are pollinated by the staminate buds, the flower closes up tight and stays that way until the following year, when the little cones start to grow. From April to August the cones grow to their full size. You can almost see them grow from day to day. Then they are ready to pick or they shed their cones.

The other conifers that we collected seed from all mature in the same season and start growing right after pollination, but we had to wait until they were all ripe before we picked them. All but the true firs start opening up their scales at the top of the cone and over several days continue opening downward, releasing the seed gradually. Each scale generally has two seeds, and each seed has a wing made of a paper-like substance attached to the end of the seed. This causes the seed to be blown a good distance away from the tree in a light breeze, and a stronger wind can blow the seed for miles. If they aren't eaten by birds or mice, they'll sprout and grow the next spring.

True firs are different in that their cones are fastened to a small, hard, woody stem standing straight up from the twig. They're formed by a flat disc around the stem, or spike, in the center called the axil. The concolor and grand fir cones are two to three inches around and three to four and a half inches high. The noble and Shasta fir cones are almost twice that size. Instead of opening up in the fall, the true fir cone discs, each with several seeds under it, start at the tip and just come apart all the way down in a week or so, leaving the axil still on the twig. We had to find and collect these cones when they were just ripe and before they started to open on the trees. We were always able to get a lot from the squirrels' caches, but I also found that by climbing and handpicking I could get a good supply.

The Douglas fir is not even close to a true fir. It was first classified by David Douglas, an English botanist who came to the Pacific Coast in 1825 on a collecting trip for the Royal Horticultural Society. He aptly named the tree Tseudosuga taxifolia, which means "false hemlock with yew-like foliage." The next people that came just called them firs, and the name stuck. The botanical name has been changed, however, to Pseudosuga menziesii after Archibald Menzies, a Scottish botanist.

My foot was definitely in the door now, and it proved to be a good entry. I had found, dried, and extracted over three hundred pounds of sugar pine seeds and two hundred pounds of ponderosa seeds. When the BLM put out a bid for seed collected in that particular BLM district where I'd gotten my seed, I bid the sugar pine in at two dollars a pound and the ponderosa at four dollars. The Manning Seed Company underbid me by five cents a pound. I lost the bid, but not for long. Mr. Peterson called to ask if I'd ever seen anyone else collecting pine cones the year before in that area. Neither I, nor any of the foresters, had. When the representative from Manning was questioned and asked for proof that their seed at been collected in the required area, he answered, "No, it wasn't, but our seed was collected near Susanville in northern California, and that's close enough." But it wasn't. Elva and I got the sale.

That was not the only way bid specification could be falsified. When tree seed is bought on a bid, samples are taken from each container and sent to the Oregon State Laboratory for testing, just as my first batch had been. Each bid has minimum specifications the seed must pass, otherwise it is rejected. The price is adjusted to the PLS (pure live seed). For years it was tested only for purity and germination, but that year the moisture content had been added. That was a big blow to the companies that had been sending in damp seed to make their containers weigh more.

As time went on I learned just how much the weather, insects, and so many other factors affected the tree seed business. Rain, fog, or even very cloudy weather can almost wipe out a Douglas fir crop. A number of years after I'd been in the business, I was asked to go to a Washington State Forest Service ranger station to see why they hadn't had a single crop of Douglas fir in the eighteen years they'd been there. The answer was simple: They were situated in a canyon near the coast where in the spring they had fog banks every day it didn't rain—this canceled out the pollen flow completely. In another case the Forest Service searched for the reason why in one area five or six years would pass without a decent Douglas fir crop, then they'd have two good crops two years apart. It was the same with all local species. The only factor that seemed to make sense is that a good Douglas fir crop usually followed a year of intense thunderstorms. This makes sense, since lightning releases free nitrogen into the atmosphere. One thing that helps a tree seed collector is the fact that seldom do all the species have a large crop the same year.

Tests have proven that the best seed crops come from seedlings grown from seed collected close to the planting site and within five hunded feet of the same elevation. One of the largest tree-seed suppliers in the Northwest proved that, though it wasn't their intention. They were notorious for dishonesty and falsely selling seed, even from Canada, saying it had come from the location required by the bid. One ranger district not far from here bought ponderosa seed from them for five hundred acres. The seedlings were raised in a nursery and planted. Fifteen to twenty years later, every tree began losing its needles. A few years later they were all dead. In the middle of that district, forty acres planted the year before with my seed was, and still is, a perfect project.

I learned something new every day, but I also believed in the saying: "A little knowledge is a dangerous thing; drink deep or taste not this Pierian Spring." I still had much more to learn. One thing I did know was that we could be much more efficient if we had a larger kiln to dry the cones in, as well as better cleaning machinery. The process was to heat the cones in the kiln with temperatures never to exceed ninety degrees, venting the hot air constantly and carefully to get rid of the moisture coming from the cones. From here, the cones went into a tumbler that shook all of the seeds out and through a mesh onto the floor, where they were swept up, sacked, and tagged as to their origin. After that, all other phases of work were done in an unheated building, regardless of how cold it was outside.

This seed, called "rough thrash," was then rolled back and forth on a mat for ten minutes, using pressure to compact it, to break off the wings. Next it was taken over to the old clipper to remove any remaining wing parts and dust, then to the link seed cleaner's hopper to be fed across a vibrating screen perforated with different size holes for different seeds. From there they fell onto another screen with holes even smaller than the seeds, which got rid of the small particles. The seeds next went into a controlled vertical air current that blew out the light particles, a slow but important step. Normally the seed went over the cleaner three or four times, because the air current was not accurate enough to separate the blind seeds from the good. Blind seeds are seeds that look like the good seeds, but for some reason the embryo didn't fully develop and can't germinate. A pound of Douglas fir seed contains an average of forty thousand seeds. You can see how hard it was to separate out one seed just a fraction lighter from the others.

So now that we made the decision to build a new kiln, we began the search for the right building materials. A local mill had stopped production and had stacks of sawed and planed eight-foot, two-by-four studs for sale. I got the idea that I could nail them in layers to make a wall three and a half inches thick to hold in the heat. We poured the frames and the slab, and I bought enough studs to build a two-story, split-level building. Our boys built forts, even two-story forts, using no nails, with some extra studs I bought for them.

I used nails, though. I bought several hundred-pound kegs of nails. I used a swing saw to saw out the knots and weak places in the studs. A neighbor gave me a hand, and the walls went up quickly. When the walls were sixteen feet, we cut rafters from two-by-sixes and used six-inch boards for the roof. We poured a slab down on the lower lever. Once that was completed, we attached a building on the south side for the tumbler room.

I especially loved tinkering with air. I came up with an airlift that astonished even me, using a principle that anyone who flies frequently enough soon learns: air can be pumped and moved at different speeds like water, but its density depends on its temperature. Flying in cold air gives much more lift than warm air. I rigged up a simple, ten-inch long vertical cylinder with air from a blower coming up from the bottom and a restriction near the top to cause a venturi—an area of less pressure—to allow the seeds to slide into the tube. It had a similar venturi on the bottom to get them out. I also designed a closely adjustable gate in the intake to allow more or less air flow. This was key, because as the day warmed up I'd have to keep increasing the air coming in to allow for lower density as it got warmer. It worked perfectly. I put a high-grade thermometer by the intake and soon learned the right setting by watching that thermometer.

One fall morning I packed my camping gear and headed toward Hyatt Lake, where I knew I could find some sugar and ponderosa pine. Mr. Petersen needed three hundred pounds of each. Since it was still pitch dark, I decided to get breakfast on the way and pick up some groceries. I took out a cigarette while I was waiting for my truck to warm up. There I was coughing up a storm while I was getting ready to light a cigarette. Suddenly it dawned on me. This is stupid! Here I am coughing because of smoking, and I'm trying to stop coughing so I could smoke another cigarette. Never once had I considered giving up smoking, but that morning I put the cigarette back in my half-full pack and drove away. I stopped in Ashland for what I needed, and went on to Hyatt Lake, where I found cones galore all day. For three days I filled sacks. Each night I'd cook a steak and vegetables. I'd sit by the fire awhile and then go to bed. By the third night I desperately wanted a cigarette. I told myself I could have one in the morning, but luckily by then the craving was gone. I carried that half pack with me for months, but never had a craving again. It's been over forty years now since I've had a cigarette.

I was a content man. The tree seed business proved more and

more to be just the right work for me. It gave me solitude, a welcome interlude, and it gave me the chance to spend most of my time in the forests and mountains, where I'd rather be than anywhere else in the world. And, too, I felt I was helping Old Mother Nature put back trees on her badly scarred land.

Ah, but by now I needed entirely new equipment. My competitors were relying on extra manpower, but I was determined we would do it ourselves. Scaling the highest mountains, crawling through jungles, none of that interested me. But thinking my way through uncharted areas to find the elusive answer, now that's exciting.

I decided to concentrate first on an even better way of drying cones. The major obstacle to reckon with was that all cones increase their girth, diameter, or circumference when they dry and open all their scales. Day and night, that's all I thought about. I always had to be alone to do my thinking, but once I had some ideas, I'd take them to Elva. She seemed to see what I'd missed, some weakness or fault in my plan, and she often had good suggestions. This time what helped is that I suddenly remembered Mr. Larabee, a farmer I met in ag flying, who had large bins with hot air blowing up from the crop dryers. Maybe he could help. And he did. (Not only did he offer me his dryers, but he wrote a letter that would get me into the largest drying operation in California, where they dried fruits, nuts, and vegetables.) "The whole secret," I was told, "is in getting the hot air up through the bins, or silos, and have it come out evenly." The answer was in the metal screens that were perforated to exactly seventeen percent of the total area. He gave me the address of the firm in Portland that furnished these.

I went home and built four long bins in our new building and covered them with the perforated sheet metal. The crop dryers blew the air up under two bins per dryer. Now my problem was how to stir the cones as they were expanding. First I tried a long-handled rake. It worked, but it was a hot job and took far too long. It took me a couple of weeks to figure out a fast, easier way of doing that. I got a cheap, quarter-inch rope, cut it into lengths a little longer than the bins, and laid them out lengthwise on the bottom of the bins and fastened them to hooks on one end. I dumped about a hundred and twenty-five bushels to a depth of two feet, spread out evenly in each bin. Once all four bins were full, I turned on the dryer. I would check after six or eight hours of heat to see if the cones were getting cramped. If so, I'd pull three of the ropes back up. This raised the height of the cones to about a foot higher, loosening them. Three-quarters of the way through the process, I'd pull the last three ropes. By now they'd have risen to about four feet. If the blowers were off, I could hear the crackling sound of the scales releasing the seed. This process was so much better than the old way. There was no comparison.

It was a long day's job to get the dry cones out and to the tumbler, so to make that easier and less time consuming, I made a device out of mostly wood that slid on top of the bin sides. It had a blade going down to within an inch of the bottom of the bin that was hinged so that it would fold up when being pulled back across the top of the cones, or dig in when it was pulled the other way. I made a sheet metal trough on rubber wheels, which was placed at the open end of the bin and filled by the blade. The full trough of cones was pushed to the end where the tumbler was, and the cones were slowly swept into the chute that fed the tumbler.

The next year there was an almost total lack of cones, which meant I had more time to work on improving my equipment. I constructed a tumbler with separate screens that screwed on so that I could change them for different size seeds. I used four-inch diameter steel tubing for the central shaft, and because bearings of that size were hard to find, I made them out of end-grain Douglas fir. I'd seen old-timers do this before. The RPM was the most important consideration. I tried all sorts of speeds before I got it correct at nineteen and a half RPMs. The angle of the slope was also critical, but I got it all worked out. That improvement paid off in the future.

The following year was so successful that it took us well into spring to get all of our seed processed. For the third time I was going to have to enlarge our kiln and cleaning equipment. What we needed most of all was a better de-winger and a more efficient way to remove foreign material from the rough thrash before it went into the seed cleaner. I chose to work on the second need first. I needed at least three different sizes of wire mesh for the seeds to fall through, and I needed to be able to change the mesh quickly. That was the hardest part to design. I bought six identical bicycle wheels at Sears, mounted them in pairs three feet apart on a light wooden framework of thin pieces of wood between the wheels, and covered the framework with hardware cloth mesh—one with three quarter-inch mesh, one with three-eighth-inch mesh, and one with half-inch mesh. I mounted the pairs of wheels on rollers on two iron shafts sixteen inches apart. One shaft was powered with a slow RPM motor and the other turned easily. I put a light tub under the wheels two feet off the deck, and a small trough to carry the rough thrash into the end of the roller, which separated the seed from the larger pieces. Now the result would flow through the seed cleaners.

Most of the powered equipment I used had to operate at a critical speed. Thanks to adjustable pulleys and different RPM motors, eventually, after much adjusting, I was able to get everything timed perfectly.

Next came the airlift. It took me a long time to figure how to get the feed to work correctly with different speeds for different seeds. When I did, I was surprised at how simple it was: The flow of seeds had to be constant or it would blow out many good seeds. It had been the interruptions that had been causing the problem.

About then, the BLM and the Forest Service announced that they were going to direct-seed from helicopters instead of planting seedlings in clear-cuts. They'd done little experimentation, but they were intent on going ahead. Theoretically, it should have worked. After logging, some of the ground is cleared to bare soil by dragging logs across it. For a conifer seed to sprout and grow into a seedling, the seed must lie on bare soil, and it can't be placed more than a quarter of an inch underground. Conifers have epigeous germination. You can't poke a hole in the ground and drop a seed in as you would to plant corn.

The experiment went on for seven or eight years before the project was abandoned. First they dispersed the seed by the slipstream of the helicopter. Practically every seed came up, but the complaint was that the swath was too narrow and too much seed was wasted. After that they mounted a propeller under the helicopter with the idea that the propeller would widen the swath by scattering the seed further. What they didn't know is that the propeller slapped the seed so hard that what should have germinated ninety percent came out less than seven percent. It would have worked if they'd used pine seed, but Douglas fir seed is much too delicate to be whacked by a propeller. The only other thing that could explain their failure would be if good seed had been swapped for poor seed. There was always that chance, since Europe was paying much more for Douglas-fir seed than anyone in the States. In fact, England now had the largest manmade Douglas fir stand in the world.

There are two showcases where seed was planted successfully by the helicopter slipstream method, happily—both with my seed. One is northeast of Salem and the other is on a mountain northwest of Jacksonville.

Dr. Lee Hunt, a friend of mine who was with the BLM, tried to point out erroneous methods to his superiors, but he was frequently ignored. A case in point was when he told them their trees weren't germinating because they weren't planted deep enough. They were being J-rooted—planted in a hole too shallow which bent their roots upward. Roots need to grow down. Since workers were paid by the number of trees they planted, they'd put them in as quickly as they could, regardless of how it should have been done. Some of these workers planted sixteen hundred seedlings a day. I planted deep and carefully, and the best I ever did was four hundred a day, and that was pushing it.

Once I was listed as a tree seed dealer, I began getting inquiries about some of our native trees and their seed. One letter came from a nurseryman in Holland requesting some Brewer's spruce seed, a fairly rare tree found only in a small area in southern Oregon and northern California. We call them "weeping spruce" because some of the ends of the twigs form long, thin, needle-covered hanging strands. I've measured some of these strands at over nine feet. Weeping spruce grow mostly on the sides of steep, rocky cliffs at high elevations. In the wind they look like hula dancers. The year I received the request was a good cone crop year. I went out in the wilderness, camped out, and returned with several bushels. I sent some seed to Holland and some I sold in small lots all over the world. The seed was for ornamental purposes, not lumber production.

I also got a request from a Mr. McKlean in New Zealand asking to buy a few incense cedar seeds for his arboretum. I put them in a matchbox and sent them off. I heard from him a year later saying they'd all been good. Years later I met someone from New Zealand who mentioned that he lived next door to a man named John McKlean who'd planted a wonderful collection of incense cedars. "I have no idea where they came from, though," he said, "and now John is dead."

"Come over here," I told him, "touch this tree. It's the parent of all those incense trees."

I don't have a record of the total seed count the next year, but I'd guess I delivered over a thousand pounds of cleaned seed to the Forest Service in Placerville. When the superintendent of the nursery got the test results from the sample seeds, he asked how I managed to get our seed collected in such numbers. Since he asked, I told him. I said for one, they needed to look at the many ways they were killing the seeds, and secondly, they were operating under too many faulty ideas for cone collection and seed processing.

For one thing the BLM and the Forest Service were treating their seeds with a number of poisons before sowing them to deter them from being eaten. It didn't work. Then they thought they'd found the solution in a poison called Endrin. "No bird or animal would touch a seed coated with that," they promised. The Forest Service in Portland was experimenting with Endrin and asked if I would help them. Since it was spring, my slow time, I'd agreed. All I needed was my cement mixer and plastic tarps to dry the seed on. They furnished the Endrin, the fine aluminum powder, and the adhesive to hold the Endrin on the seed. Elva and I worked outdoors, wearing goggles, face masks, and gloves, while we coated several thousand pounds of seed that year.

I was curious, so I put some in our bird feeders. For three or four days nothing happened to the seed. I thought maybe there was something to this, until I noticed some of the bright aluminum seeds had been broken in half and the inside kernels were gone. I tried it again several times before I was certain that this scattered seed would eventually all be eaten despite the Endrin.

Five years later I had an occasion to meet the head chemist for Ortho Garden Chemicals and asked him about Endrin. He laughed and said he'd tried it, too, but it was an extremely unstable chemical. Anything over a three degree temperature rise in an hour will cause the main ingredient to disintegrate, making it no longer toxic. I told the Forest Service what I'd learned, but they still continued using it.

Elva and I found other things to dry besides cones. One was the Chimaphila umbellata, the Common Prince's Pine, also called Pipsissewa. It grows in our coniferous forests and in parts of Europe, and has been used for centuries as a medicinal herb. In those years when we had no cones, we'd send our pickers out to collect these. After we dried the plants, they had to be baled for shipment, most of which we shipped to the Western Crude Drug Company in Portland. The leaves and roots have a bitter but refreshing taste. Elva and I still chew the green leaves when we're out in the woods.

Arthur, their oldest son, describes his involvement with this endeavor, as well as some other jobs the boys were given: There wasn't much work to do in the summer except to stomp Pipsissewa, and that wasn't much fun. Pops had all these empty bins, so he figured why not use them to dry pipsissewa and sell it to the people who use it to make root beer. Pops knew where it was growing. He was very observant, always watching and remembering everything he saw. He'd driven all over the place looking for cones, so he knew exactly where to take us to do the picking. The leaves, stems, roots, and flowers all went in to be dried. Then they had to be baled. Mom and Pops would put the plants in a huge gunnysack and throw us kids on top to jump up and down and stomp it all down tight. Then they'd throw in more dried leaves, and we'd have to keep this up until the sacks were filled and packed as tightly as possible. It might sound like fun, but it wasn't. We were hot, sweaty, and just plain miserable. We had to learn to sew the sacks too.

Pops bought mountains of old, used gunnysacks from the Lebanon Bag Company, and the last thing he wanted to do was to clean old grain out of his new seed, so that was our job too. We had to turn those sacks inside out and shake all the grain out of them. Breathing in all that dust out in the hot sun wasn't much fun for a ten-year-old.

He reused his seed bags, too, so we had to check through thousands of them looking for holes and snags. Then we'd lay pole boards down crossways and put the bags over them to dry, otherwise, they'd rot.

Sometimes on weekends in the fall we'd go cone picking. Pops also hired local families and migrant workers to pick. They could earn a hundred dollars in a weekend, which was far more than they earned in two weeks at the mill. In 1966 they were earning less than three dollars an hour in the sawmill. One of the migrant workers, a loner and a little looney but an excellent worker, told my dad, "In all my life I've never made money like this, and I've never been treated so fairly." Everyone that worked for him felt that way. My father's philosophy was cast in stone. He'd show them what to do and what he expected. If they did their job well, they'd be well paid. He never had much patience with people who wouldn't accept responsibility for their own actions, though. He didn't tolerate our whining either. He was a hard worker and he made sure we knew the meaning of the word. In the fall, during tree seed season, we had to work after school and weekends, many times until well after dark.

When we didn't have to work, we were left on our own. We grew up like wild Indians in the middle of nowhere. The only rule we had was **BE HOME BY DARK.** *And we were! We had to listen and do what we were told. Pops worked most of the time, though he would take us up in the woods and teach us how to survive, but we never did things like other families. He didn't have time. He took us fishing, but once we knew how, we were on our own.*

School was important to my folks. There was no question but that we had to get through. Mom would help us with our homework, but Pops was too busy working and inventing. He never settled for anything less than perfect. He'd read and pick other people's brains, and then work on a problem until he came up with the solution he wanted. He set records in seed germination that haven't been broken today. He taught himself , and he designed and made his own equipment. I've always admired his perseverence. It didn't matter what area he was working in, he always looked for perfection. Tim gave him the name Pappy Lems because often Pops would come up with a lot of lemons before he was satisfied. But then, so did Thomas Edison.

The one thing my brothers and I looked forward to all year was the Fourth of July. All year we saved our empty quart juice cans. We'd poke a little hole in them with an ice pick, and then on the Fourth we'd fill them with water and take the 250 Savage, the .30 -.30 or the .45 - .70 and shoot them. Boy, those cans could really blow up. It was Pop's idea.

You know, he never could do anything ninety-nine percent, it had to be a hundred and ten percent.

Tim, the youngest of their three boys, said: Dad was always busy. Discipline mainly came from Mother, but when Dad got involved, we were in big trouble. We had few neighbors. My entertainment was with my brothers. Vacations and playtime were few and far between. Dad had just gotten into the seed tree business about the time I was old enough to be aware. I didn't understand then the time it takes to start and run a business. He never tried to get us involved in the tree seed business, though we had to help out with chores like picking up and moving heavy bags from one place to another.

He sold his airplane in '59, I think, and I only got a couple of rides when I was a kid. He did get us involved in riding motorcycles once he sold the plane. I spent most of my childhood on a motorcycle.

I marvel at Dad's talent. He made all his own machinery. All of his tools were off limits to us kids. He didn't show me how he did things, but I guess I've inherited his talent. I'm creative and I like building stuff. I'm self-taught, too. I have a lot of him in me.

If I had to describe Dad in one word, I'd say "creative." And he's synchronized with nature. He follows nature's example of how to organize and translates the principles into the mechanical. He's an absolute genius.

In the summer of '62 International Paper Company asked me to harvest seed from their land north of their Mt. Shasta plant. It was a clear, sunny October day and we were just getting started, when a wind sprang up from the south. Within twenty minutes it reached eighty miles an hour, blowing over big trees and filling the air with flying debris. The winds slowed down about dark, and the next morning we could see the destruction everywhere. Nearly every treetop was broken off and had blown away and hundreds of trees were gone. Two of my pickers were trapped by downed trees in the mountains near the Kalmiopsis wilderness area. They had to walk eighteen miles before finding help. Weeks later they went back for their pickup and had to saw eighty-nine large trees to get it out of there.

It was such a bad year for cones that International Paper canceled their order. The following year was also a bad year since so many of the treetops, where the bulk of the cones were grown, were gone. Nature has a clever way of dealing with losses. A limb under the break will turn its growth to a vertical direction instead of horizontally and become the new top.

Elva and I took advantage of the poor crop year and began building our new house. I also had a road bulldozed in. In my spare time I'd work on clearing the land, which was really one big rock pile. We built our split-level house using Douglas fir logs, which are the heart of the fir logs that have been peeled to make plies for plywood. We got them from a local mill with dovetail ends for joining, and grooves on the tops and bottoms to fit into each other. Holes were drilled at sixteen-inch intervals down through the logs for a cable to be passed through to fasten to the concrete footing. Elva and I did our own footings, but we hired a bricklayer to put up the blocks for the lower half of the building. We put our own logs together, much like Lincoln logs, and had a cone picker help with our roof. We also put up the Sheetrock and then hired a carpenter to do the finishing work and an electrician to do the wiring. When we moved in, we still had no flooring down and no painting done. Elva had wanted to wait until the house was completely ready, but I was too eager.

According to Elva: Our house still isn't finished. He was always working, creating, and inventing, but the house wasn't first on his list. Actually, Tom moved in even before I did. The minute the stove was in, in he went. I didn't. It was still full of sawdust and dirt. We made a door for a deck, but to this day I still don't have a deck. He always said he was going to put an elevator in, but that hasn't happened either. We built three bedrooms downstairs for the boys. We thought it would be fun to make it like a jail, so we put bars on the doors with numbers. Tom was going to be the supervisor and I was going to be the matron. Well, we never got around to that either. He wouldn't let me have a washer and dryer down there, which was the only place in the house I could have put one. He said it would clutter up the hallway. But you know what? The boys got to keep their motorcycles there, and I had to go to the laundromat to do our wash until after they grew up and left. Then I got my washer and dryer.

Our business was growing so fast that we had to move some

of the seed equipment into the old house. Once again I had to enlarge my equipment.

Sometimes we gave cash prizes to our pickers for the best average seed count. Elmar, from Estonia, and Peeler, a migrant fruit picker, were usually the winners. The Manning Seed Company set up a buying station near us, but because of their lower prices, they didn't get any of our pickers. Our pickers knew we were honest and we knew they were. A couple of times Elva made a mistake in their favor, but they always brought it back to be corrected.

The 1964 cone season lasted into November. Our drying sheds were full of sacks and there were hundreds more on the ground. Our kiln was running day and night. A week or so before Christmas it began to rain hard, a typical South Pacific low-pressure front. It continued raining hard for a couple of days and then turned into a cloudburst of warm rain. The mountains had their usual couple of feet of snow, which soon melted, and the creeks and river began rising fast, higher than we'd ever seen. When I hurried to save the sacks of cones down below the old house, I found John, fourteen years old then, swimming out and back with a sack at a time. We saved a lot of them, but lost eighty-three sacks.

The noise from the storm was tremendous. The river was full of debris—floating propane tanks, furniture, you name it , every inch was filled with something. We'd see the big old trees shake and before long they'd disappear. Almost all of them went in one day. A huge log jam farther up the river broke loose, and warnings were issued over the radio to alert the people on the bridge. Our electricity was out and so was our phone, so we couldn't call anyone, but a policeman got word to the twenty-five people watching the storm from the bridge, saving them just in time before the log jam let go.

The next morning the two-story house we could see by the bend in the river was gone. There had been dozens of houses there, but now only one still stood, and that had serious damage. Elva took some good pictures of the devastation. The river hadn't reached our house, but it did reach the foundation, and where there had once been a solid row of trees on both sides of the river, now there were only two big cottonwoods and a stump on our side. Trees have since come back, but not to the size that we lost.

I was already running late with my seeds, and now our three phase lines were down for several days, so I couldn't operate the kiln. The following day six inches of snow gave us a white Christmas, but there wasn't much cheer for those who had lost everything. Once I was back in commission, I began a series of working long days and many nights, not leaving the place for one hundred and forty-four days. The flood had washed out all but one bridge across the river between Shady Cove and Grants Pass. Our neighbors across the river had to go to Grants Pass to cross over and back—an eighty-mile trip to the east side of Shady Cove. Since that was too far for the children to travel to school, the government provided a jet boat for their transportation. Most of us had never heard of a jet boat before. By the time I finished running the seed, the jet boat was gone and the Army had built a temporary bridge across the river.

Soon after that I got a letter from Washington asking if I'd be interested in being a consultant for the US Forest Service. If so, I was to take the letter to Truman Puchbauer, the district ranger in the Tiller District in Oregon. I met Puchbauer, who seemed delighted I was going to help him out. It was a new area for him, a large forest, and he'd been ordered to make a major seed collection. As it turned out, I would only have been a hired man, not a "government-issued slave." Since I'd had no formal education, Puchbauer pointed to a man raking leaves and said, "I can't pay you any more than I'm paying him then." I told him I wasn't about to falsify my records, but since I had some time anyway and I'd like to explore his district, the largest in the state, I would agree to the minimum wage and the standard mileage for furnishing my own vehicle.

In fact, Tom had been giving talks on cones and tree seed collecting at the Society of American Foresters' meetings, speaking to people with university degrees. His own education background had never been mentioned. When offered an honorary degree from the Society of American Foresters, he refused, saying once again, "If I'm not welcome in the front door, I'm not going in the back"

Since I was covering the entire area, driving the full length of all the roads in the district, I used my favorite back-road car—a Volkswagen Beetle. It was on one of those trips that I found a grove of large maples that later gave me some of the best music wood I ever had. It has since been made into wonderful instruments by some of the best makers in the world.

In late August of that year we collected several years' supply of Douglas fir cones, the most predominate and most valued species in that area. The ponderosa pine made a poor showing, but we got a bumper crop of incense cedar. The incense cedar cones are different from the others. These cones have inch-long pods with two seeds in each, sometimes four, and that year some even had six. Normally, the radicle, or primary root, in the seed is in the end of the seed opposite the wing. In the incense cedar and the western redwood the radicle comes out of the other end. Because of that they can't be de-winged; the radical would break off and the seed wouldn't sprout. We were careful to tag the sacks with a notice: **DO NOT DE-WING**. The following year I returned to see how we'd done. All the collections were good except for the incense cedar, which had been de-winged in the new sixteen million dollar seed extractory owned by the US Forest in Wind River, Washington.

In the meantime, the BLM and the Forest Service had stopped seeding by helicopter and had gone back to trying to raise seedlings. This so reduced their requirements that I didn't see much future in continuing. We sold the business to a local man. He paid a nominal rent for the buildings for three years until he bought land of his own and moved the equipment.

Chapter 16

Music Wood

It was my friend Raddy Gardener's brother who got me interested in the violin wood business. Victor Gardener had made some violins and was looking to find local maple and spruce to make more. He had already found a small maple with the necessary figure, called a flame or curl, and another had been found when it was cut down to make way for a bridge, so he knew they were in the area. When they asked me for help, I took them to an area where I'd seen a number of maples. I did this for them several more times, before it dawned on me that I was doing the work, but I wasn't getting a dime for it. The wood I was finding was valuable and expensive. I decided then and there I'd do well to look more seriously into the 'tone wood' for stringed instruments.

I read everything I could find on the subject. I knew where to find the wood, but I had no idea how to pick the good trees or how to saw them to very exacting specifications. I didn't want to waste any of this valuable wood. Elva bought me my first good chain saw, a Stihl 0.41, which I still have today. I designed a device to bolt to the chain saw that allowed me to accurately slice the pieces of wood for the violins, violas, and cellos. Then I got a permit to buy a tree from the Forest Service. I sawed the wood and put it in one of the cone-drying buildings. The wood had to be dried for five or six years before it could be used. I also contacted several dealers in my area to let them know what I was doing.

Tom refused to go into detail about the way he selected the best trees. "It's a trade secret," he said, "and since my son John is still running the business, I see no point in passing on information that would help our competitors."

Victor Gardener is also responsible for making our "Tepper wood" well known. Victor had traveled to Italy to visit his father's home town. While he was there he visited the Italian School of Instrument Making at Cremona and the German School at Mittenwald, Germany, showing my wood at both places. Soon after I received a letter from David Wiebe, an American student at Mittenwald, asking if I could send him a couple of pieces of the spruce wood. After Wiebe returned home to Nebraska, he came to meet me in Shady Cove and chose about a dozen tops, backs, and necks for his work.

A year or so later, Wiebe entered a viola he'd made from Tom's wood in an international competition. Distinguished musicians played the instruments and judged which was the finest. According to Wiebe, he had no notion that he was making an instrument of any consequence. He'd dressed casually, inappropriately apparently, because someone approached him saying, "Don't ask me why, but I urge you to change your clothes." To Wiebe's astonishment his viola won the Gold Medal. He had so little hope of winning that he had filled out a job application for driving an asphalt truck and was going to turn it in after the competition.

Fortunately for Wiebe and Tom, there were other musicians at the competition who'd heard his instrument played. Instantly he had orders to make more. Among those musicians was Claude Kenneson, the well-known Canadian cellist, who gave Wiebe the order for his first commissioned cello. And it was the well-known violist Donald McInnes who eventually bought the Gold Medal winning viola and later played the world premiere of the then newly commissioned William Shumann Viola concerto in Avery Fisher Hall with the New York Philharmonic during which Leonard Bernstein used that viola. Donald McInnes has since played that viola in London, Paris, and other major cities. Through Donald McInnes, Yehudi Menuhin became acquainted with Wiebe's work and wanted him to make instruments for him. In fact, it was a viola Wiebe made that Menuhin used for his recording of the Brahms Viola Sonatas. Since then Wiebe has made other instruments for the late Lord Menuhin, as well as for the late Leonard Rose, famed cello solist and teacher at Julliard; Claude Kenneson; Zara Nelsova, famed cello solist, and many other well-known violin, viola, and cello players. Wiebe's instruments have found homes all over the world, including one on permanent display in a museum in Peking, China.

Claude Kenneson spent three days with us here in Shady Cove, along with David Wiebe. David was choosing wood to make Kenneson a cello. While they were with us, Kenneson practiced for an hour every day in our house. His playing was perfection. When he invited us to come to a musical festival in England, I was deeply honored, but I knew there was no way I'd ever go. I've never owned any pants except for jeans. I can just see myself attending that festival dressed as I always do.

In a letter dated 19 August 1996, Claude Kenneson related his own account of David Wiebe's award and his visit to the Teppers:

With my late wife, the distinguished violist Carolyn Kenneson, I attended the International Viola Congress on the campus of Eastern Michigan University at Ypsilanti in June of 1975. At that time she was performing on a magnificent early viola made by David Wiebe after his return to Nebraska following his study at the famous violin-making school (Staatliche Fachschule furGeigenbau) in Mittenwald, Germany. Because a violin making competition was planned for the Ypsilanti Congress by the American Society for the Advancement of Violin Making, David Wiebe decided to enter this viola. The result was that Wiebe was awarded the Diploma of Honor, and this brought him international prominence and commissions from such artists as William Primrose and Yehudi Menuhin. I remember with pleasure that he went on stage with William Primrose to the ecstatic applause of the crowd. He was both joyful and dignified on that great occasion.

Carolyn Kenneson continued to perform on this diploma viola ("Mighty George" was her whimsical nickname for the instrument), appearing later that summer as soloist for the Purbeck Festival of Music in England. In the fall, the instrument became the concert instrument of the outstanding American violist Donald McInnes.

At that time, I was playing on an eighteenth-century cello—an instrument made around 1720 in Cremona by Vincenzo Ruggeri—that had been owned by the great European cellist, David Popper. But inspired by Wiebe's work, I commissioned a new cello shortly after the Congress. In the early summer of 1977, during a break in my schedule of recitals, Weibe and I set out for Shady Cove where I would meet the Teppers for the first time. Our intention was to acquire the best possible wood for the newly commissioned cello.

My three days in Shady Cove were unforgettable. Because I had been privileged to know many wise men, I realized immediately that Tepper was an exceptional man. I particularly remember sitting with him in the woods as he spoke about the trees he so loved and respected, demonstrating a remarkably perceptive grasp of the nature of this great resource and explained some of his observations that had led men like Wiebe to admire him. "See how that old maple bends in the wind—up there eighty feet or so? That elasticity at that point of its flexing promises something great for a violin. . .wood from that section will vibrate like a Stradivarius violin." or, "I'm a humble man. If I manage to leave my footprints in the sands of time, it will be because I have lived in these woods and observed nature at work, and have become a part of violin making."

Because I had recitals ahead, I practiced everyday in the Teppers' living room. They both admired music and respected musicians, so they often listened as I worked. He was particularly intrigued with my ancient instrument. And we ate together and chatted about life. And career pursuits. They were eager to hear about my decade of work in England where I had appeared at summer festivals, notably the Purbeck Festival in Dorset and Cheltenham Festival near Bath, where I had performed new music by many contemporary composers, including Sir Arthur Bliss, at that time Master of the Queen's Music. I invited them both to hear the new Wiebe cello once I began to perform on it and, if possible, to come to England some summer and enjoy the music festivals.

During January and February of 1977, Wiebe made the new cello in his workshop in David City, Nebraska. It was completed and sang its first musical sounds on 1 March 1978, an unforgettable day for me. On 25 March I played on it in public for the first time in performances of Saint-Saens' cello concerto. It has been my concert instrument ever since and is now in its eighteenth year as a cello, although its wood probably lived for a century in Oregon before Wiebe crafted it into a musical instrument.

I remember with great respect my final evening at the Teppers' home when they announced that they had a surprise for me. He left the room and returned with some very special wood for the new cello. This particular prime spruce and maple had grown to maturity a few miles away. (The tree stumps are still there.) This marvelous wood had formed part of Elva's special collection and had been in keeping for years, pursued by many cello makers because of its natural perfection and finally handed to David Wiebe for the project at hand.

David Wiebe at work on a violin using Tom's wood.

Claude Kenneson with his cello.

Clockwise, from left: Tom with a handmade pickaxe; Elva with one of Tom's walking sticks. She is seldom without one; Tom dragging home saplings to be made into walking sticks; young saplings waiting to be whittled, sanded, stained, and rubbed into walking sticks.

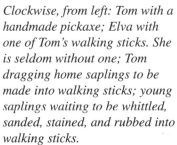

Tom making a walking stick. He refuses to sell them, preferring to give them away. Because he expresses interest in having his walking sticks in as many different countries as possible, the co-author carried a stick to Holland and one to Belgium where she found it is not an easy job to give something to strangers. Eventually, trusting and receptive people were found, who corresponded with Tom.

For a musician, such memories never fade. Even now as I handle the magnificent Wiebe cello of 1978, I remember my first memorable glance at its wood when it was handed to me for my pleasure in Shady Cove at the Teppers' home in 1977.
Sincerely, Claude Kenneson

Dealing in wood can be confusing, and early on I learned I needed to know more than just a little. A good example is that Acer pseudoplatamus is really a maple, but because platamus means plane, and the plane tree is a sycamore, I often got requests for sycamore from the English when what they wanted was maple. Pseudo means false or look-alike. Acer pseudoplatamus means a maple that looks like a sycamore. Also, the Europeans call 'Picea abies' a pine when it's really European spruce, so they ask for pine when they want spruce.

The bottom and sides, or ribs as they're called, of the instrument are made of maple, with variances in thickness but not in overall dimensions. So are the neck and bridge. The top with the 'F' holes is made of spruce. The fingerboard and pegs can be of ebony. Inside the ribs, where they're bent, small blocks of willow wood anchor the ribs in place. A strip of spruce, called the soundbar, is glued to the top inside to alter the tone. I've had good makers tell me that they carve out the top so thin in places that you can see light through it. Naturally, all of the best makers have their own secret methods. You don't ask them questions, especially about the finish or varnish they use.

While some folks like crossword puzzles, figuring what the stock market will do, or which horse will win the Kentucky Derby, I like the mysteries I find in the forest. That is my true home. Not much money there, but lots of satisfaction. I remember a beautiful old spruce we found that had been struck by lightning and had its top fifty feet blown off. Knowing it couldn't live much longer, we got a permit to fell it. It was by far the oldest tree we'd ever cut down. We counted the growth rings carefully. The last fifteen years of rings were so close that it was difficult and slow counting, but John and I decided it was either four hundred and eighty-nine or four hundred and ninety years old. We cut it in 1980, which made it just a baby when Columbus came. Think of the history in that one big spruce that gave us many good tops for our instruments.

One of the best trees we got had been scorched on one side when loggers had pushed their slash pile too close. The Forest Service sold it to me for the minimum cost of the permit—ten dollars. That spruce provided us with some wonderful tone wood that's now playing music in many different parts of the world.

Sometimes we came across surprises while we were hunting for wood. Once, John and I were following and sampling a scattering of maples, when a well-dressed young woman suddenly stepped out in front of us. "There are lots of rattlesnakes around here," she warned, "you better not continue there." We could see a large green tent sent up in a clean, neat campsite surrounded by six-foot fir seedlings. She was on vacation and camping there with her cat, she said, and her brother lived in the area. I could see John was barely able to contain a laugh. As soon as we left, I asked what he'd found so funny. "Those weren't fir seedlings," he said. "Those were marijuana plants, about as big as they get." He was right. We went back the next spring and the 'fir seedlings' had disappeared. I've seen lots of those plants since—I just keep on walking by.

After many, many hours of carrying wood out on a packboard, I decided to make the job easier. I made a light but strong travois with a single motorcycle wheel under the center instead of runners on the rear, and two handles on each end. It took two of us to operate it, but on a smoothed-out trail we could carry a hundred and twenty-five pounds a trip.

Music wood is greatly influenced by the site it grows on. If asked, most people would say that trees grown in good soil with an adequate water supply and enough sunlight for good transpiration would supply the best wood. This makes sense, but it ain't necessarily so. Humans, animals, and even trees are hardiest if they have learned to cope with hardships. This is apparent in some of the qualities in tone wood.

After we've cut out a back or top and air-dried it, we'll hold it gently in exactly the right place with thumb and forefinger and tap with our knuckles. If it's good, it will resonate. This is easy to demonstrate, but hard to describe. Instead of just a thump, the sound will be prolonged, like a thummmp, and you can hear it a good ten feet away. Finding the right tree takes time and patience as well as knowledge. For every good tree I've taken, I've looked at and sampled hundreds of others. This means crawling through some gosh-awful thickets of brush and up and down steep ground. We call it our factory, but John, who took over the business in 1979, and I both love it. The air is always fresh and there are no exhaust fumes or the sounds and smells of factories. I stay out of the tone wood business now that John has taken over, except to help him fell a tree. The big hardwoods are difficult to lay down just where you want them, so it's helpful to have someone to drive in the wedges at exactly the right seconds.

Of his father, John says: Pops has always been in charge of the direction he has taken in his life. He'd take a subject and dive right into it. He'd live it, absorb it, and get everything he possibly could out of it. He could focus on only one thing for as long as he needed to. He needed to KNOW. He has this incredible thirst for knowledge, a curiosity, an appetite that is never satisfied. It was never for the purpose of earning money. Money never has meant anything to him. The fun for him is in the learning. Once he's got it, he's on to something else. He always has to have something new to grow on. That's always been the most important thing to him.

Our life was not like the lives of most kids. We never took vacations. Oh, I remember one time we went to the coast, but that's the only real family vacation we took. We had motorcycles, and my dad and my brothers and I would go riding, but Mom had to stay home and take care of things there.

I treasure the times he'd take me up behind our place to hunt. And he gave me my gift of wings, and that's always been special to me. May 28, 1978. It took him about a month to teach me to fly. I was a slow learner, I guess. Mostly we learned by being around him, though I probably spent more time with him than my brothers did. They had other interests and went off and did their own thing. I wanted to be with him. He's definitely an interesting man.

The only 'lickin' I remember him giving me was when Tim and I tried to straighten a wooden rifle he'd made for us. It had warped and we thought we could bend it back in shape. It didn't work!

After the service I got involved in the wood business with Pops. I got to know him real well then because we'd hike and explore the woods for hours together. I give him all the credit for having the ideas of how to do something and figuring it all out, but when it came to the commercial part of business, he felt, "The hell with it." He didn't want to be involved with that part. Also, he didn't want to deal with the people. Luckily, I like that part. Certainly, working together was at times like two women working in the kitchen—we both had our own way of doing things. He's not involved with the wood business anymore, so I have my own way now. It took me a long time to come to that. For years I'd back up everything I said with, "My father told me."

Now I'm older and I know I have to be my own person. Pops is an honest man. He wouldn't take a penny from anyone. If you call him at three in the morning and say your roof just blew off your house, he'd get right up and be there to help. Just a few years ago we had a big fire up in the mountains behind us. I grabbed my shovel and headed up. It was quite a climb, and when I got there the firemen, who'd come in a different way, couldn't believe I'd gotten up there so fast. Before long, here came my father with his shovel—up the same way I'd come. He was over eighty years old and still climbing the mountain to fight fires. He put in many of the paths the firemen have used to fight the fires around here.

I have a lot of respect for the old man. You know, he has a spiritual side that he keeps to himself.

It's been an incredible life. I have to admit that I never had a goal other than to get out West. Once I'd realized that dream, I guess I just sort of let life happen. Certainly my direction was influenced most by what I loved doing, and first and foremost what I loved doing was running around in the woods. Secondly, I loved learning. I love a challenge—looking for better, easier, and quicker ways of doing things. I don't believe I could do that without the peace and quiet to think for long periods of time. I guess that's why I've been called "the hermit of Rogue River." I love my solitude.

Recently I heard a broadcast from London with Yehudi Menuhin (just before his death) playing a duet with one of his proteges. My eyes filled with the thought that this great violinist was playing such beautiful music thousands of miles away on wood that we might have chosen. He'll never know now that this old man who provided the wood for his instrument was the same man who listened to him play when he was just a young boy. That this same man, then in his twenties, couldn't afford the twenty-five cents admission, so he listened through the partly-open backdoor.

Chapter 17

The Evening Years

Tim, Elva, Tom, Arthur, and John Tepper.

Now that I'm retired and my eyes won't let me engrave silver as well as I used to, I've started wood carvings, where the patterns are larger and easier to follow. As one old artist told me, "Laying out designs is easy. There are only two kinds of lines that you can make—a straight line or a curved line." I didn't have any woodcarving tools, so I sent away for a few, but then I began to make my own. I have well over a hundred tools now, most of which I made. It's a challenge and a feeling of accomplishment to take a piece of steel, heat it up in my forge, hammer it out, harden and draw the temper and then sharpen it. This way I get the exact angles I want. I made one of my favorite tools in four different sizes.

Many carvers prefer wood that's easy to carve, but I like it harder. It takes longer to carve, but hardwoods can produce much finer detail. Some carvers who use softwood soak it in glue so it doesn't crumble away. I rate madrone as being good. Yew is fair to good for carving, but very good for lathe turning. White alder seems to have slipped through the cracks and is seldom used. The red alder, found over much of western Oregon and to the north, has also been ignored. Here in southern Oregon we have more white alder than red. I'm surprised that it hasn't been used more, because it details very well. I can carve a little bird out of it and the beak stays on without glueing. Our big-leaf maple is a very good carving wood, too. Altitude makes a difference. Trees that come from up near the timberline have a much denser grain, which means they require more detailing.

I make staffs for people who hike into the hilly country. Now that I'm old, I take one with me because I don't want to fall. A staff of the right length and shape for handholds can save a lot of leg work; it acts as a third leg. My staffs are scattered all over the country now, and even in Europe. It takes me two days to make one. I use hand tools except for the knobs on top, which I turn on my wood lathe. For the knobs I use various hardwoods, most all of them from scraps of tone wood.

Tom would love to have his staffs in as many countries as possible, and, as this writer mentioned in the beginning, he doesn't sell them, he gives them away. So. . . in an effort to help him realize his dream, I offered to take a couple with me on a trip to Holland and Belgium. If you've never tried to give something away, especially to people who don't speak your language, and vice versa, I warn you that it's no easy task. Vigorous head shakes of no and a quick get-away was the usual response. No one believes someone would give away something unless there's something costly, illegal, or threatening involved. It took dozens of tries before I was able to accomplish this, and then only because the man, whom I'd seen limping, turned out to be a visiting Canadian who spoke English. He accepted one for his Dutch relative and one for himself. Tom has been corresponding with the Canadian ever since he wrote to Tom telling him how much he loved and appreciated his gift. Belgium will have to wait.

I still do a lot of hiking. I need to be among the trees. I've always wanted to be buried with the trees surrounding me and where few people pass by. I want the same solitude in death that I've enjoyed so much in life. The best use for my body when I no longer need it will be to improve the soil where a tree can use some substance from the part of me I'll be leaving behind. I did some research and found that in our county I can be legally buried on my own property. With Elva's help, it's all arranged. The site of the grave had to be described and filed with the title company, recorded in the courthouse, and a copy given to the sheriff's office. We have thirty-six acres, with two sides adjoining government land. It's too steep and rocky to farm or to be useful in any other way. I chose a site close to some oak, pine, and fir trees, and I dug my own grave. It was hard soil to dig in—real pick and shovel work. Rocks, roots, and clay. I worked about four hours a day, and it took me two weeks to get down to six feet by three feet. I had a shock on the last day. I was at the bottom and I had it all cleaned out—but I couldn't get out. I had nothing to hold onto on the top and no ladder or anything. Fortunately, I still had a heavy crowbar in the grave. I propped it up and was able to reach the shovel handle, which I used to pull an old five-gallon can over into the grave with me. I stood on that and was able to rescue myself.

Elva says: Tom asked me if he should dig a grave for me right beside him. I told him, "No indeed, I've spent fifty years with you. Now I want to be free." I also told him to leave room for all his catalogues and magazines so I can throw them down there with him. Living with Tom hasn't always been easy, but it's sure never been boring.

> The clock of life is wound but once
> And no one has the power
> To move the hands to late or early hour.
> So live and love, toil with a will,
> Place no faith in time,
> For you the hands may soon be still.

Author unknown, but a favorite and often quoted poem by Tom

Epilogue

Tom died October 16, 2002, the day after his 92nd birthday. He was not buried in the hole he had dug. Elva preferred to be cremated and scattered up in the hills above their house, where they loved to hike. Tom decided he'd rather be with her.

John brought the can with his father's ashes home, put it on his workbench and said, "Now, get back to work old man." And there Tom waits until he and Elva take the trip up the hill together again.

Should one wander into that workshop, one is likely to find a single fresh flower draped over that can.